A Public-Sector
Journey to Lean

A Public-Sector Journey to Lean

Fighting *Muda* in Times of *Muri*

Kate McGovern M.P.A., Ph.D.

A PRODUCTIVITY PRESS BOOK

First edition published in 2019
by Routledge/Productivity Press
711 Third Avenue New York, NY 10017, USA
2 Park Square, Milton Park, Abingdon, Oxon OX14 4RN, UK

© 2019 by Taylor & Francis Group, LLC
Routledge/Productivity Press is an imprint of Taylor & Francis Group, an Informa business

No claim to original U.S. Government works

Printed on acid-free paper

International Standard Book Number-13: 978-1-138-54275-4 (Hardback)
International Standard Book Number-13: 978-1-351-00824-2 (eBook)

Library of Congress Cataloging-in-Publication Data

Names: McGovern, Kate, author.
Title: A public-sector journey to lean : fighting muda in times of muri /
Kate McGovern.
Description: 1 Edition. | New York : Taylor & Francis, [2019] | Includes
bibliographical references and index.
Identifiers: LCCN 2018030487 (print) | LCCN 2018033633 (ebook) | ISBN
9781351008242 (e-Book) | ISBN 9781138542754 (hardback : alk. paper)
Subjects: LCSH: Government productivity—Measurement. | Six sigma (Quality
control standard)
Classification: LCC JK1525.P67 (ebook) | LCC JK1525.P67 M34 2019 (print) |
DDC 352.3/57—dc23
LC record available at https://lccn.loc.gov/2018030487

Visit the Taylor & Francis Web site at
http://www.taylorandfrancis.com

and the CRC Press Web site at
http://www.crcpress.com

This book is dedicated to Sam McKeeman who

started us on our Lean journey.

With grateful acknowledgment of all the amazing public servants who have

contributed to this story. Thank you for being an inspiration. Lean on!

Contents

About the Author

 **Kate McGovern**, MPA, Ph.D. is a Lean trainer and practitioner. While working for New Hampshire's Bureau of Education and Training (BET) in 2009, Kate was inspired by a Lean course taught for BET by Maine's Sam McKeeman. Along with her colleagues at BET, Kate designed and presented a series of Lean training programs and joined in the development of a Lean Network in New Hampshire. She has participated in regional Lean events, both as a speaker and trainer. She assisted in the development of a Lean training program for the Vermont Agency of Transportation through Daniel Penn Associates, and has conducted training for the New England States' Government Finance Officers' Association (NESGFOA) and served as the coordinator of New Hampshire's Lean Black Belt program.

Prior to her Lean work, Kate served as BET Director and Associate Professor in the Certified Public Supervisor and Public Manager programs. She has worked as an adjunct faculty member at Springfield College's School of Human Services, a public information officer for the New Hampshire Retirement System, and a field representative for SEIU Local 1984.

Kate holds a BA from the University of Connecticut, an MPA from the University of Hartford, and a Ph.D. from Fielding Graduate University. She is the author of *Challenges in Pension Governance: A Case Study of the New Hampshire Retirement System*.

Kate's family includes her supportive husband, Michael Dumond, who was the first to read all 10 chapters of this book. Between them, Kate and Michael have five daughters, Michelle, Amy, Emily, Christina, and Katie. Kate can be contacted at katemcgovern@cox.neta.

Introduction to Lean, *Muda*, and *Muri*

I first learned about Lean while working for the State of New Hampshire. My colleagues and I had no idea that it was a management system—we just thought it was a really cool way of making our bureaucracies more efficient. We traveled a path of discovery, benefiting from the insights and experiences of other practitioners.

Like most new students of Lean, we learned a few Japanese terms to describe the key concepts. The most commonly used term is *kaizen* (*kai*, to change, and *zen*, to make better), which describes Lean activities ranging from specific projects to a broad cultural understanding.

Lean practitioners also learn about the three Ms: *muda* (waste), *mura* (unevenness or variability), and *muri* (overburden). Beginners in Lean generally focus on the removal of *muda*.

The impact of *muri* is not as readily understood. However, it is extremely significant for those of us working in government. Decisions on staffing levels and resource allocation are made by elected officials who are generally disconnected from daily operations. Short-sighted cost-cutting makes it difficult to deliver quality services as efficiently as possible. The mantra of "do more with less" creates ever-increasing *muri*.

In contrast to robust Lean programs in privately owned companies, efficiency initiatives are regularly cut from public sector budgets. Antiquated systems remain in place, with too few workers to operate the existing processes. The debilitating impact of persistent *muri* brings burnout and turnover, perpetuating a vicious cycle.

Despite the *muri*, a dedicated cadre of public servants is hard at work using Lean techniques and principles to break down bureaucratic red tape and improve the quality of services at every level of government across the country. While I've incorporated examples of Lean initiatives in other states to give readers an idea of all the terrific work that is occurring, this book is really the story of one of those journeys.

Using our New Hampshire experience, you'll learn about our steps along the way. Each chapter tells a story of what we did, what we learned, and how the lessons can be applied. I've included annotated outlines of our White,

Yellow, and Green Belt programs, and our Lean for Leaders workshop, as well as two hypothetical scenarios that we've used as training exercises. These approaches are not intended to be authoritative or prescriptive; they are offered as insights and examples.

You'll read about the challenges and pitfalls, and the creative countermeasures developed by our dauntless team of Lean practitioners. We hope that sharing our story will inform and encourage others.

Material based on the New Hampshire Bureau of Education and Training's Lean programs is included throughout the book. Since Lean is neither copyrighted nor are Lean skills formally credentialed by an accrediting body, our White, Yellow, Green and Black Belts are colloquial credentials.

As you see our journey unfold, readers may notice that we developed the Yellow and Green Belt programs prior to the White Belt. Ours, like some other Lean initiatives, started with classes about process mapping techniques; subsequently, we added classes about other Lean tools and principles. Only later, as the program was taking hold and growing, we realized the importance of a broad introduction to Lean for the entire workforce, so we created a White Belt component. Ideally, a White Belt or "Lean 101" class would be required for all current staff and part of the orientation program for all new employees.

In the spirit of *kaizen*, we are continuously improving these programs. As our Lean community grows, so do the innovations to our practice and our pedagogy.

White Belt	An overview of Lean concepts and techniques preparing participants to identify opportunities for improvement projects in their organizations.	Origins are described in Chapter 5 Program agenda is in Appendix A
Yellow Belt	A hands-on introduction to the philosophy and methodology of Lean process improvement. During the 3-day class, participants apply *kaizen* process mapping techniques to an actual work process and construct an implementation plan to enact the improvements.	Program material is in Chapter 2 Hypothetical class exercise is in Appendix B

(Continued)

Green Belt	Facilitation and change management. Participants prepare to become Lean practitioners and learn how to guide a group through a *kaizen* event, while considering the challenges of organizational change. Following the 3 days of classes, students will participate in a required practicum. *Pre-requisite: Yellow Belt.*	Program material is in Chapter 4 Facilitator instructions are in Appendix C and a class exercise is in Appendix D
Lean for Leaders	A 60–90 minute workshop that prepares directors and administrators for their role in Lean initiatives and Lean management. Available for agency management teams upon request.	Program material is in Chapter 7

1

Getting Started

INTRODUCTION TO LEAN

Since the term "Lean" was first used by a team of MIT researchers studying the Toyota Production System, Lean principles and techniques have spread across the globe. An Internet search will generate many definitions and descriptions, such as "Lean means creating more value for customers with fewer resources."[1] It's more than a set of tools and techniques to identify and eliminate waste—it's an operating principle for smooth flow and standard work. Most importantly, it's a perspective—a way of thinking. It's not an acronym; it's just a word. The "L" is not always capitalized. It's not copyrighted; there's no patent on Lean methodology—the field is wide open for growth and innovation.

My preferred definition comes from a paper produced by the Government Finance Officers Association (GFOA). I like it because it expresses the multidimensional aspect: "Lean is an organizational performance management system characterized by a collaborative approach between employees and managers to identify and minimize or eliminate activities that do not create value for the customers of a business process, or stakeholders."[2]

The approach to continuous improvement in manufacturing has been adapted to finance, health care, and government. When Lean entered the public-sector decades after its proven effectiveness in manufacturing, its core concepts remained the same, with the same transformative potential as in private industry. However, the challenges differ due to various manifestations of *muda*, *mura*, and *muri*. Lean practitioners are most familiar with the Japanese term *muda* (waste), and perhaps less so with *mura* (unevenness, variation) and *muri* (overburden). *Muri* is a significant factor impeding Lean implementation in the public sector, and therein lies a tale.

1

STARTING THE JOURNEY

Fledging Lean efforts generally start with process mapping, and our start was no different. Here's the story:

Shortly after his appointment to lead New Hampshire's Department of Environmental Services (DES) in November 2006, Tom Burack became the chair of the Commissioners' Group. Tom and a core group of other commissioners were using a collaborative leadership model to move beyond the individual fiefdoms to an era where they could operate as a single enterprise to serve the citizens of the state.

The first initiative was directed at customer service training (2007), which naturally lead to Lean process improvement (2008), given Lean's focus on value for the customer. The following sentence was inserted into the list of job accountabilities for every job description in State service: "Recognizing that everyone we come in contact with is a customer; consistently treating all with courtesy, respect and professionalism; striving to exceed customer service expectations; and maintaining harmonious work relationships".

The Commissioners' Group heard about Lean's potential in a presentation by then-state representative David Borden. Prior to his service in the NH legislature, David used Lean principles in the hospitality industry. He described his philosophy in his book, *Perfect Service*:

> First, we adopt the view that people are basically good, that they are capable of greatness, and that the environment we create for them—the systems, knowledge, and skills—can bring out that greatness….Focusing on people's innate goodness is an incredibly powerful management tool.[3]

David worked with Commissioner John Barthelmes of the Department of Safety (DOS) and DOS Chief of Policy & Planning Kevin O'Brien to respond to customer complaints in the Division of Motor Vehicles substation in Manchester by organizing the first Lean event in a state agency.

David recalled how bad things were prior to the Lean initiative: "The DMV substation in Manchester had requested a state trooper to maintain order among frustrated driver's license and automobile registration customers. Often people had to wait 2 hours only to be told that they had the wrong paperwork. 'Don't worry deary,' the beleaguered clerk would say, 'when you get back just come to the front of the line and I will handle it'… Kindly service, horrible process. Now the staff, with the help of two highly placed Department of Safety employees, have totally redesigned the processes and the state trooper is back at his day job. The lines have disappeared and one of the staff was not replaced when she retired."

Improvements included cross-training of employees between registration and licensing. Customer wait times were reduced, and the frustration of waiting in the wrong line was eliminated as counter clerks were prepared to assist customers with either transaction. The customer feedback approval rating for the DMV went from 35% to 95%.

Confident of its potential, the Commissioners' Group was eager to move forward with Lean. Fortuitously, DES received an Innovation Grant from the EPA, and Tom asked the State Bureau of Education & Training (BET) to arrange Lean training. BET Director Dennis Martino recruited Sam McKeeman, a trainer whose Lean work for Maine's Department of Transportation had resulted in $310,000 of savings in the first year of the program. Tom invited his colleagues from other departments, including Transportation (DOT), Safety (DOS), Administrative Services (DAS) and Health & Human Services (DHHS) to attend Sam's training, and to bring selected staff members.

The first class in Lean Process Improvement Techniques included several of us who would soon become a cadre of Lean activists. Sam introduced us to process mapping and we immediately saw the potential as several projects unfolded over the 5-day session. The DES project on issuing administrative orders (AO) was particularly promising. The future state workflow would reduce the process time for AOs from 18 steps to seven steps, changing the process from 114 days to 14 days. Another project reduced a permitting process from 16 steps to 5 steps.

Our multi-agency group of participants was eager to begin cutting the red tape that plagued our working lives. We were bitten by the Lean bug. Although we knew that overarching improvements would require legislative action or permission from risk-averse administrators, it was an incredibly empowering experience to see that we could make a start.

Commissioner Barthelmes (DOS) sent two staff members to attend the training: Roberta Witham, a statistical analyst, and Christopher Wagner of the NH State Police. The duo had not met prior to Lean training, but they were both chosen to lead the effort at DOS. Roberta recalled the Commissioner saying, "This is the way we are going to revolutionize Safety: learn and make process improvement happen." After the training session, she and Chris had a brief "crap—what do we do now?" moment, but quickly adapted to their new mission. They established a pragmatic working model for Lean at the DOS; clearly the Commissioner had made the right call by selecting them to lead the initiative.

Roberta saw the need to do short *kaizen* events with tangible results. She joked that people knew they would retire before the seemingly never-ending efforts to redo the state's aging IT system could be accomplished. Chris agreed that they should start with small, significant wins, noting that "we're not trying to solve world hunger." Taking a pragmatic approach, they targeted processes that could be improved by 80%, understanding that they could go back to the other 20% another time (Sam had recommended an 18-month interval for revisiting projects.)

Armed with rolls of brown paper, colorful sticky notes, and a can-do attitude, the new Lean practitioners put the lessons to work. They tackled one of the most onerous processes in New Hampshire State government: the preparation of contracts for review by the Governor and Executive Council (G&C). An examination of the current state found that more than 70% of the contracts prepared by Department of Safety were returned for rework. The Lean project identified several points of failure. For example, some of the reviewers would only read far enough to find one error, so the documents were returned with one item fixed, only to be sent back again as additional errors were subsequently identified. The team identified training needs and established standard work. After project was implemented, 92% of the documents were accepted on the first submission (Figure 1.1).

With continued support from the Commissioner and Chief O'Brien, Chris and Roberta conducted a series of Lean projects. They developed a model for Lean teams to work of 4 half-days, followed by the presentation to the sponsor ("the sell"), which would take place early in the following week. While some of the team's recommendations might be approved at the sell, the sponsor would have two weeks to respond to the entire package.

Early successes included reducing the amount of returned mail to the DMV from 18% to 2% (It was not possible to move away from mailing altogether due to a post 9/11 requirement to mail the applicant's driver's license to the home address on record.) In addition to the staff time spent on the project to design the future state and conduct training on the new workflow, the DOS spent $2,500 on software for address confirmation, resulting in a $225,000 saving in postage costs.

Department of Administrative Services (DAS) Commissioner Linda Hodgdon encouraged Lean training with real workplace projects for several work units within DAS. The Public Works unit mapped their

FIGURE 1.1
Roberta Witham and Christopher Wagner present the results of their G&C project to a Lean class (2009).

consultant selection process using swim lanes (as depicted in the graphic that follows). By reducing the interdepartmental handoffs and other *muda*, their process went from 36 steps to 15 steps. A process that had taken 6–9 months was reduced to save 80 days per project—in many cases, they saved a construction season (Figure 1.2).

DHHS Commissioner Nick Toumpas supported a hub of Lean activity generated in the Office of Integrity and Improvement led by Linda Paquette and subsequently by John MacPhee. Lean efforts at DHHS took on a larger, long-range approach for several significant projects. Rather than the quick-hit style *kaizen* event used at DOS for 4 half-days, DHHS Lean practitioners attempted to get to the root cause of some of the most vexing processes. Two of these projects began during training sessions, but were too complex to be completed in the 5-day session with Sam: contracting and rule-making. The projects each took more than a year, with small wins along the way, and a larger win at the close.

In 2014, John unrolled the current state value stream map of the contracting process at a meeting of the Governor and Executive Council. Following that meeting, the council agreed to increase the threshold amount of the contracts required to be sent to them for review from $10,000 to $25,000.

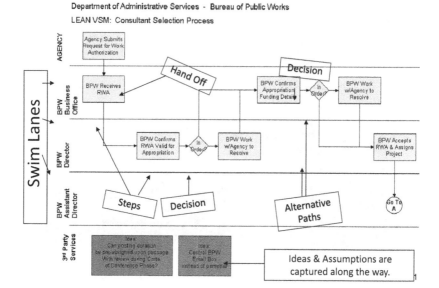

FIGURE 1.2
DAS project on the consultant selection process.

An early attempt to lean the rule-making process took even longer than the contracting project. The project was championed by Representative David Borden, who had worked with Chief O'Brien on the project at the Manchester DMV office. In 2009, David recruited six of his fellow legislators to attend one of Sam's training sessions. During the hands-on portion of the training, the legislators worked with a staff member from Legislative Services to map the rule-making process. It was a particularly challenging project: rules are drafted by staff in the dozens of departments within the Executive Branch, then subject to review by staff attorneys in Legislative Services, as well as a public comment period, before receiving final approval by the Joint Legislative Committee on Administrative Rules (JLCAR). Despite many snags along the way, the project resulted in the passage of legislation that reformed several aspects of the cumbersome process.

Below are excerpts from the data sheet used in that initial session. Sam introduced us to the types of measures used in manufacturing, including "up time," "change over time," and "first pass yield." There's a simplified version of the data sheet in the next chapter, which we adapted for our administrative processes. It was, however, useful to learn about Lean through a manufacturing lens. The "first pass yield" indicator reported that rule adoption at JLCAR meetings was estimated at 60% during 2009.

The other interesting indicator was an estimated annual cost of $225,400 for agency personnel attending JLCAR meetings. Staff was expected to be available in case any of the legislators on the committee had questions.

Step Name: JLCAR meeting	**# of Staff Involved**: The number of people doing this step at the same time from the Agencies and Boards: 3–26. Average of 11 per agency
Annual Staff Time: Multiply the number of people doing this process by the average time each spent	165 person hours/year with travel time = 245 person/hours per year
Annual Staff Cost: Amount of staff time in hours multiplied by the cost of staff per hour @ $46/hour	$11,270 per agency; ×20 agencies = $225,400/year
C-T Cycle Time: The amount of time it takes to complete this step measured from the end of the previous step to the end of this step	If the document goes in on Wed. and the next meeting is in 15 days, the average cycle time is 15 days; however, for those items held over to next meeting, it would be with 30–45 days
V-A Value Added: An estimate of the % of value added to the customer by this step	Value provided runs from 0 min to max time answering questions (30 minutes?). Average could be 2 minutes?
C-O Change Over: The amount of time it takes to change over the mindset, paperwork, machine or program from the last product of the previous set up to the first product of this process	Time that agency staff needs to stop what they were working on before going to JLCAR and time to get back and reset to useful work (could run from 30 min–2 hours)? Average 45 min
U-T Up Time: The % of time the person, program, printer, etc. is available compared to the time needed	1–2 days; 6–7 hours per day over the course of 1 month (14 hours/720 hours) ≤ 2%
FPY First Pass Yield: The % of time that this process is done correctly the first time through	If there is carryover because the wrong person came or the right person was there, but meeting ran over time (estimate 4 of 10 times) 60%

One proposed countermeasure was to allow staff to bring their laptops and work in an adjacent room, while they waited for their agency's item to come up on the agenda.

Each subsequent training session generated more projects. In early 2011, a team from the Appeals Unit of New Hampshire Employment Security needed to solve a significant problem: the time elapsed for adjudication of appeals was the longest in the country. Pending appeals clogged the system, in part due to the convoluted administrative process and system, and in part due to new software that logged certain inquiries as appeals. The spike in layoffs during the Great Recession compounded this problem.

Appeals unit administrator Erika Randmere organized a team to attend training, including one of the hearings officers, the agency's training manager, the clerical unit supervisor, and a member of the clerical staff. Following the redesign of the workflow, the unit met federal standards for the first time in years, going from 50th to 16th in the country for case aging.[4]

Metrics		
Percentage of appeals processed in 30 days	6%	86%
Average age of a pending appeal	164 days	18 days

While training classes continued to be the primary opportunity for *kaizen* projects, Lean projects were also underway onsite in the agencies that had sent personnel to Sam's training. Due to differences in culture, structure and capacity, different agencies used a variation of the Lean techniques that were presented in the training. For example, DOS' paramilitary structure established clear expectations for compliance. The Commissioner and Chief O'Brien's commitment made it possible for Chris and Roberta to conduct 27 Lean projects at DOS and another 14 in collaboration with other agencies, from 2009 to 2016. Lean practitioners at most of the other agencies were unable to convene the staff necessary to serve on Lean teams, or to have the management support to implement changes. Budgetary limitations were also a factor. Few of the other agencies would have been able to spend the $2,500 for the software that enabled the project on returned mail to save $225,000.

NONSTANDARD WORK

In late 2009, commissioners from DES, DOS, DAS, DOT, and DHHS approved a charter for the Lean Statewide Standardization Committee "to develop standardized Lean documents, templates, training, glossary, approach to analysis, and metrics and to make that toolkit readily available statewide electronically." The committee had Lean practitioners from each agency who would rotate the duties of hosting and convening meetings. Decision-making was by consensus. As a practical matter, under-resourced, collaborative structure was not up to the task. Unable to wait for a committee to achieve consensus, each agency's Lean program developed somewhat differently.

Without a statewide Lean coordinator, the effort to develop a standard approach to Lean was abandoned early on. The differences were acknowledged in training, so the new Lean practitioners would be prepared to adapt to the program's approach in their agencies. They were also encouraged to consider integrating good ideas from others.

John (DHHS) and Roberta (DOS) were frequent guest speakers. They presented alternative approaches to Lean in a lighthearted segment dubbed "the John and Roberta show." Roberta would encourage the trainees to be bold in their choice of projects and their pursuit of Lean, and to avoid being discouraged by naysayers, urging them to "proceed until apprehended."

Although agencies without funding for training were left behind, agencies that trained staff and subsequently allocated time to continue Lean work moved forward.

With the ongoing support of the commissioners of DES, DOS, DHHS, DOT and DAS, our group of Lean practitioners built a Lean Network. We began meeting on a regular basis to share best practices and offer mutual support. While some had the blessings of the top leadership in their agencies, others attended with permission from their supervisors.

The Network grew in fits and starts. After many successful projects at the agency level, practitioners were building confidence and expertise. In 2012, the Network expanded to include representatives from the New Hampshire Army National Guard and then-Governor John Lynch sent a staff representative, Liz Gray, to join the group and to assist in organizing the first Lean Summit, with the governor taking a lead role.

The governor asked agency heads to bring their management teams and the event drew 300 people. Each of the agencies with an active Lean program had a display table. The governor chaired a panel discussion by Lean practitioners from the private sector, a municipality and a non-profit organization. He awarded a proclamation to the team that had moved New Hampshire from 50th to 16th in the country for processing appeals (Figure 1.3).

SUMMARY OF LESSONS LEARNED

Getting started: There must be a champion, like Tom Burack, with sufficient commitment, influence and access to resources to get something

FIGURE 1.3

NHES team recognized by Governor John Lynch at the Lean Summit on September 18, 2012. Pictured: DES Commissioner Tom Burack, DHHS Lean facilitator Bill Baggeroer, and NHES staff Lis Izarrualde, Greg Ives, and Renee Carboni.

going. Most organizations hire consultants or external trainers to assist in launching their Lean initiatives, like Sam McKeeman. When using an external resource, the organization needs the capacity to transition from the outside expert to an ongoing internal program. At that point, the consultant could be asked to provide a "train the trainer" program, and the organization might be able to purchase the rights to use the consultant's materials.

The transition from Sam McKeeman's work to the development of training by the New Hampshire's Bureau of Education and Training was particularly smooth. Since Sam also worked in the public sector in Maine, his materials were not copyrighted, and his collegial relationship with BET Director Dennis Martino provided the opportunity for ongoing support for the fledging Lean efforts. Martino credited Sam's enthusiastic and encouraging style. "He did not approach Lean in a dogmatic way with an abundance of rules. There are no 'Lean Police.' We owe him a huge debt of gratitude. He energized NH's first zealous Lean practitioners."

Moving forward: Differences in technique are not insurmountable. Lean coordinators from each agency can work together to develop a common approach and promote best practices without insisting on uniformity. The lessons that Sam taught in 2009 were adapted to fit the culture of each agency as they developed their Lean programs. While certain principles remain at the core, the tools and techniques may be applied differently, as we'll see in the next chapter. As Sam explained, "Lean works because the learning never stops."

APPLYING THE LESSONS

- Launching a Lean initiative requires a champion with vision and commitment who has the influence to recruit others to the cause, and access to sufficient resources to initiate a training program. The training should be open to staff from all agencies, regardless of the agency's ability to pay.
- Management at all levels must support the new Lean practitioners by sponsoring projects and by providing time for the early adopters to form a community of practice. And that's just getting started— there's much more for management to do that will be described in later chapters.
- Make the program visible. Start a website with photos of Lean teams and announcements for training and other events. Start a blog.
- The optimal training program format incorporates theory and practice—teaching Lean principles and applying Lean techniques. Ideally, the program will provide the opportunity for participants to conduct real projects, demonstrating proof of concept and creating a cadre of early adopters. The Lean Yellow Belt program is described in detail in the next chapter.

NOTES

1 "What is Lean?" Lean Enterprise Institute. Accessed February 13, 2018. www.lean.org/WhatsLean/.
2 Shayne Kavanagh and David Krings, "The Eight Sources of Waste and How to Eliminate Them," *Government Finance Review,* December 2011: 19.
3 David Borden, *Perfect Service* (Magna Publications, Inc. Madison, WI, 1994) 54.
4 The New Hampshire Employment Security Appeal Process. Case Study. 2011. Accessed August 8, 2018 http://lean.nh.gov/Documents/ProjectCaseStudies/department%20of%20employement%20security_rev.pdf.

2

Follow the Yellow Belt Road

This chapter describes the introductory training program. It also notes where there may be differences among Lean practitioners in terminology and methods. It's not surprising that the growing community of practitioners have different styles and approaches. As the use of Lean continues to expand into sectors beyond manufacturing, Lean tools and techniques are constantly evolving.

The lack of standardization may seem somewhat paradoxical, since standard work is one of the core tenants of Lean. However, the principle of continuous improvement coexists with standard work, as the improved product replaces the previous product. It is in this spirit that we developed our Lean Yellow Belt training.

This program has evolved since 2009 and continues to do so, as our practitioners and trainers continue to learn and innovate. Resources specific to public sector efforts are extremely helpful. The EPA's Lean in Government Starter Kit[1] was one of our early favorites. We have also benefited greatly from networking with public sector colleagues in other states.

When the Yellow Belt program replaced the initial "Introduction to Lean Process Improvement Techniques," it retained a hands-on approach. Former BET Director Dennis Martino explained, "Training was never abstract or theoretical. It was specific and concrete. Teams went away with knowledge; it is true. However, they walked away with a useful product too."

Learning objectives are in three general categories: understanding of Lean principles and tools, skill building in *kaizen* process mapping, and preparation to apply the lessons in their workplaces.

The typical Yellow Belt class runs for 3 days. Six of the 18 hours are comprised of instructional periods, interspersed with 12 hours applying Lean techniques to a *kaizen* project. The classroom sessions are at 9 am and 1 pm each day; each session serves a dual purpose—to acquaint participants with Lean principles, and to provide instruction for the upcoming phase of their *kaizen* project.

Participants are encouraged to enroll with four to six colleagues who share a work process that they can "lean" during the hands-on portion of the training. Those who enroll as individuals without a project team will be assigned to join other teams as "fresh eyes"—to help the teams identify waste in their processes.

For a class of 25 participants, three projects work simultaneously in breakout rooms. Tip: Have a hypothetical project prepared for classes that don't have three real workplace scenarios. (There is a sample project in Appendix B.)

Each of the teams is guided by a Lean facilitator. This serves a dual purpose—it's a great way for rookie facilitators (Green Belts) to practice and for seasoned facilitators to expand their range of experience.

The remainder of this chapter covers the Yellow Belt program in three sections: first, the class agenda; second, the lessons about Lean principles, tools, and techniques; and third, the lessons to guide students through the hands–on component of the class.

PART I. AGENDA FOR THE 3-DAY LEAN YELLOW BELT CLASS

Day 1
9:00–10:15 Classroom session

- Introduction to Lean—Definition, history, core concepts
- Preparation for hands-on project: briefing on chartering, identifying the customer, constructing team ground rules.

10:15–10:30 Break.

10:30–12:00 Project work. Class breaks into teams. Those who enrolled as individuals will be disbursed among the project teams—they will have the role of "fresh eyes" helping their teams to take an objective view of the process. Each team develops ground rules, reviews a draft charter, prepares a problem statement, and identifies the end-user customer. They post the ground rules, the problem statement, and the customer on flip chart paper.

12:00–1:00 Lunch.

1:00–1:45 Classroom session

- Topics: monuments, the 5 Whys, examples of successful Lean projects
- Briefing to prepare for project work: Mapping principles and techniques.

1:45–2:45 Project work—current state mapping.

3:00 Tour of the projects. Each team selects at least one "tour guide" to describe the project to the others in the class. The participants move from project to project, noting how each map tells a different story, and asking questions of the team.

Day 2

9:00–9:45 Classroom session begins with the instructor asking each participant to comment on the experience on Day 1 or any other observations about Lean. Classroom topics include root cause analysis, assessment of value, and measurements. Teams are introduced to the data sheet tool.

10:00–12:00 Project work—teams continue current state map and work on data sheets.

12:00–1:00 Lunch.

1:00–1:45 Classroom session on Lean concepts of smooth flow, standard work, and quality through design. Teams are briefed about future state design and implementation plans.

2:00–4:00 Project work—teams complete the data sheets, tally the current state metrics on flip chart paper, and begin to work on the future state.

Day 3

9:00–9:45 Classroom session with an overview of Lean concepts and tools including Plan-Do-Check-Act/Adjust (PDCA), the A3 template, the 5S (system for workplace organization), and Poka-Yoke (mistake-proofing). Teams are briefed about resistance analysis and developing a communication plan.

10:00–12:00 Project work—teams complete their implementation plan and prepare their "sell" to their sponsor. If time permits, they summarize their A3 report on flip chart paper.

12:00–1:00 Lunch.

1:00–1:30 Classroom session on continuing with Lean, including information about the NH Lean Network and the Lean Executive Committee.

Participants from organizations without active Lean programs are encouraged to work with management to start one.

1:30–2:00 Project work—final preparation for presentations.

2:00–3:45 Project presentations. Teams using real work place projects are encouraged to invite their sponsors to view their presentations. Teams without sponsors may use a proxy sponsor or present to other teams in the class. Teams are encouraged to view at least one other team's presentation.

3:45–4:00 Closing, presentation of certificates, course evaluation.

PART II. OVERVIEW OF THE YELLOW BELT PROGRAM

Classroom presentations prepare the participants for the hands-on project work, beginning with definitions and background.

Lean is

- A set of techniques to identify and eliminate waste,
- An operating principle to simplify and standardize,
- A perspective and a way of thinking.

Initially developed for use in manufacturing processes, Lean is now widely practiced in the nonprofit and public sectors. Characterized as "common sense uncommonly applied," Lean methodology provides a set of tools that assist in the identification and steady elimination of waste, improving the flow of work processes. As waste is eliminated, quality improves while time and costs are reduced.

Lean is built on certain assumptions: all work is a process, most processes have about 95% non-value-added time, there are reasons for inefficiencies, and formal efforts are required to reduce waste.

Lean work teams optimize process performance by implementing incremental change, steadily and consistently, by using the intellectual capital of the employees who are responsible for doing the work. The number of process steps is normally reduced by 30%–40% in the first effort. With an ongoing practice of Lean principles, many processes can potentially realize a time-saving approaching 90%.

The Lean philosophy is about creating value for the customer while using the fewest resources. It's about getting the right service in the right amount to the right person at the right time, while minimizing waste and being open to change and improvement. Lean is a way of thinking to adapt and continuously improve.

Lean is not an acronym. It's low-tech and user-friendly. Lean done right will build morale, enhance teamwork, and encourage innovation.

The Alignment of Responsibility and Authority at the Lowest Possible Level

The assembly line in American manufacturing was an innovation in the use of smooth flow and standard work. Toyota added the component of customer value by designing an innovative management system. Unlike the hierarchical management structure in the U.S., where frontline workers were treated as extensions of the machines, Toyota engaged the entire workforce in principles of continuous improvement.

The contrast between hierarchical control and shared responsibility is core to understanding Lean. The appropriate alignment of authority and responsibility is exemplified by the Andon cord. When the cord is pulled, the assembly line stops. Workers in Toyota plants have the responsibility to stop the line when an error is noticed, so that it can be addressed. In contrast, workers under traditional management would need to ask permission to stop the line. Even if a supervisor could be contacted in time, the line might need to keep moving to maintain production volume. Traditional manufacturing relies upon the quality checks at the end of the line.

Lean principles empower workers with the expectation that they know their jobs and they share responsibility for quality. The Lean mantra of "accept no defective product, make no defective product, pass along no defective product" is operationalized by the fact that any worker is expected to stop the line if something is not right. In Lean management, all workers are responsible for product excellence. Quality is enhanced when the people who do the work are engaged in continuous improvement, rather than delegating the role to supervisors or quality control (QC) units.

The transition to Lean is not intuitive to those who have always worked in system of hierarchical management. The shift is equally challenging for those at the top who think they are required to have all the answers, as it is for frontline workers who believe that they are powerless over inefficient systems.

Students in Yellow Belt classes may claim that they know how things could be done better, but "'they' won't let us make changes." In a Lean system, "they" becomes "we" as quality becomes everyone's responsibility; workers have ownership, and management has trust.

Kaizen

Kaizen is a combination of two Japanese words: *kai*, meaning "to change," and *zen*, meaning "for the good of all." *Kaizen* is founded on the belief that small, incremental changes routinely applied and sustained over a long period result in significant performance improvements. The *kaizen* is a short, 3- to 5-day event to evaluate a process that affects customers or stakeholders, consumes significant internal resources, or is frustrating to employees because it is clearly not working as well as it should.

Among the scholars and practitioners who have contributed to the development of continuous improvement management systems, W. Edwards Deming (1900–1993) is perhaps the most notable. His work as a consultant in Japan following World War II facilitated the resurgence of the country's industrial base and set the conceptual foundation for what became the Toyota Production System. Deming's publication, *Out of Crisis*, described his theory of management, including his 14 Points for Management.[2]

The Yellow Belt program integrates several lessons from Deming's work, including Point #8 "Drive out fear, so that everyone may work effectively for the company."[3] He understood that if employees believe efficiency improvements threaten their jobs, they will not be enthusiastic participants in Lean initiatives. Managers and employees both need to know that Lean is *not* about cutting staff. In most organizations, the list of pending projects exceeds the staff's capacity to keep up. Efficiencies gained by Lean initiatives can free up staff time to accomplish other priorities.

At the New Hampshire Department of Safety, Commissioner John Barthelmes has assured his staff that jobs may change, but employees will not lose their livelihoods because of Lean initiatives. The State of Washington's program "Introduction to Lean Thinking" explains that Lean is not about eliminating jobs or devaluating what people do. It frees people up to focus their time and talents on other quality work.[4]

The Eight Wastes

Lean in manufacturing initially targeted seven wastes: defects, overproduction, waiting, transportation, inventory, motion, and excess processing. The cost of producing unsold items (overproduction) or unusable items (defects) clearly impacts the bottom line.

In applying Lean to the service industry, the first seven wastes remained applicable, but an additional waste was identified: underutilized people. Although the semantics and sequence may vary among Lean practitioners, the eight wastes are often listed using the acronym DOWNTIME.

- Defects
- Overproduction
- Waiting
- Non-/underutilized people
- Transportation
- Inventory
- Motion
- Excess Processing.

The most significant wastes in bureaucracies are linked with the inefficient use of human talent—particularly excess processing and waiting. Administrators review work that has already been checked several times. Perhaps they will make inconsequential edits and return it for rework, adding time and effort without increasing the value of the product. Each handoff increases wait time, and each new level of review involves excess processing.

As employees work in these processes, they may become jaded and demoralized. As Deming noted, "A bad system will beat a good person every time."[5] A system filled with *muda* has an insidious impact on those charged with its operation, compounding the *muri*. It's both disheartening and exhausting. Conversely, joining a Lean team charged with redesigning the process can be a liberating experience. The underutilized human potential is unleashed.

PART III. LEAN PRINCIPLES AND TECHNIQUES FOR A BASIC *KAIZEN* MAPPING PROJECT

Instructions to trainers: It's okay for project teams to arrive at Yellow Belt training without a draft charter. They'll learn about chartering on the morning of the first day and draft their own problem statement. Below are some of the core lessons, as the project team moves through a basic *kaizen*.

Chartering

The charter is a document that defines and authorizes the Lean event. It identifies the team members, the end-user customer, and the project goals and scope. The charter also determines the bookends: the first and last steps in the process to be leaned. During the project, a team might recommend narrowing or expanding the bookends, but the charter establishes the initial scope. Team composition, time for the event, and proper project scope are all vital components that make the Lean work feasible.

Each charter has a problem statement. The team needs a clear understanding of the problem, so they agree on what they are trying to solve. Lean practitioners differ on the format and optimal level of specificity. Teams in the Yellow Belt class are instructed to phrase the problem statement as a question starting with "how."

Example: Citizens complain about the permitting process. Problem statement: How can the permitting process be streamlined so that all qualified applicants receive their permit within 10 business days?

The charter should set measurable goals for the team, based on the data about current production and service delivery levels. If statistics are not available because the process has never been measured, the team will make estimates during the project.

Examples of measurable goals:

Reduce the number of applications returned for rework from ____ to ____.

Decrease the amount of time it takes to issue a routine permit from ____ to ____.

The charter also identifies the customer(s) and stakeholders:

- The customer for the process you have selected is the end user—at the final step of the process boundary you have established for this project.
- There are also internal customers at each step of the process, as the work is passed forward.
- There may be others who benefit from this process, such as the public at large; they are stakeholders.

Charter templates vary among Lean practitioners; some are more detailed than others. There are examples of completed charters in Appendices B and D.

Description of Team Roles

Sponsor: A senior leader in the division within which the Lean event is taking place, someone enthusiastic about Lean and willing to take the risks necessary to assure a successful outcome.

- The sponsor works with the Lean coordinator or facilitator to set the goals and the scope for the project and draft the charter, assigning a team of employees, and signing the charter empowering them to redesign the process.
- When the project is completed, the sponsor meets with the team to hear "the sell" (the proposed future state of the process) and authorizes the implementation plan to make the changes needed to achieve the future state.
- The sponsor is ultimately responsible for the successful implementation of the project, removing obstacles and holding people accountable for follow-through.

Team Leader/Champion/Project Manager: Lean practitioners use different terms for this role on the team. Generally, this is the supervisor responsible for the process, and s/he also serves as a team member. During the Lean event, the supervisor has no greater say than other team members. However, before and after the event, the supervisor has additional responsibilities:

- To work with the Lean facilitator and the sponsor to set the schedule for the project.
- To coordinate the project's implementation, adhering to the schedule for team check-ins and ensuring follow-up activities take place as planned. Also removes barriers, drives accountability, and contacts the sponsor if intervention at that level becomes necessary. Celebrates milestone accomplishments with the team.

Data Manager: This role varies with different Lean practitioners. Depending upon the resources available for the project, the team may need to divide these tasks among the members.

- Manage the data sheets;
- Track research assignments;
- Update the charter, as appropriate;

- Prepare the project summary;
- Optional: prepare an electronic copy of the current and future state maps.

Lean Team Members: The employees who execute the process

- Map the current state of the process exactly as it is conducted;
- Analyze the current processes for improvement opportunities by providing firsthand knowledge of execution challenges, customer needs, and root causes of problems;
- Use creativity and insight to identify solutions;
- Design a future state, and, if appropriate, an interim state;
- Identify the tasks required for implementation, recommend staffing responsibilities and a timeline, and present those plans to the sponsor;
- Execute the reengineered processes, as approved by the sponsor;
- Take responsibility for completion and follow-through of project work assignments, measure the results, and be prepared to adjust as appropriate.

Caucus Members: Subject matter experts who join the team as needed to contribute operational expertise in areas such as procedures, technology, business controls, and legal or regulatory matters.

Lean Facilitator: The team's guide throughout the Lean process. Depending upon the structure of the agency's Lean program, the facilitator may also be involved in follow-up, tracking the implementation, confirming the improvements, and reporting the information to a Lean coordinator.

- Work with the sponsor and/or project manager (PM) to scope the Lean event, and assure that the project is set up for success;
- Provide the project team and sponsor with Lean concept expertise and best practices;
- Facilitate so the team remains focused and in scope;
- Advise on implementation and communication plans.

Ground Rules

Lean events rely on teams developing a common understanding of the way the work is currently done and designing a better way to do it. This event may be the first time some team members learn about the work of others elsewhere in the process, and the first time they've been asked for their ideas. Some team members may be eager to make changes; others may be cautious. While there is strength in diversity of perspective, it needs to be managed constructively. Before the mapping starts, the Lean facilitator works with the team to develop ground rules. Some teams adopt standard ground rules, while others construct their own. There are two essential rules: "leave rank at the door" and "no blame."

1. Leave rank at the door. Cross-functional teams can only be successful if all members feel safe to speak up, regardless of their status in the organization. Typically, sponsors and/or members of upper management are not on *kaizen* teams. Some practitioners have a firm rule against sponsors being on the team. Others believe that involvement in a *kaizen* event would allow top managers to understand how Lean functions and to contribute collaboratively to the development of a future state. If there is a sponsor or top administrator on the team, the facilitator must manage the situation to avoid three primary risks: that they dominate the conversation, attempt to steer the team to a predetermined solution, or that staff are deferring to them.

2. No blame. This rule is particularly important because the team will be evaluating the value of each step. The facilitator must remind the team that value from the customer's perspective is not a value judgment about the employees' work ethic or professionalism—it's about the process.

Typical ground rules for a Lean event:

- Leave rank at the door: one person-one voice, regardless of position;
- No blame—this is a blameless environment;
- Keep an open mind to change;
- Everyone on the team participates;
- Maintain a positive attitude;
- Stay focused—support the facilitator's role in guiding the group;
- Don't leave in silent disagreement;
- Practice mutual respect—do not interrupt, and there are no dumb questions or ideas;
- Offer honesty;
- Say ELMO (enough, let's move on) if appropriate.

Don't forget that the small stuff matters. Each team should discuss and agree on appropriate conduct and housekeeping rules. For example: don't interrupt others, don't text or take phone calls in the room (step out if it's an emergency), and be sure to take breaks.

Optional: Select a team name. Some facilitators also ask the team to select the name of a favorite vacation spot to use as a code word for a light-hearted way to call out ground rule violations.

Process Mapping

Process mapping is a visual tool that outlines every step required to provide a service or product to a customer. The Lean team will use the technique to document the current state exactly as the process is conducted now, and to design an improved future state (Figure 2.1).

Materials for a *kaizen* mapping project: large sheets of paper (typically 8–12 feet), colorful sticky notes, markers, painter's tape and regular tape, data sheets, flip chart paper.

Guide to making the process visible:

- Tape a large sheet of paper on a wall.

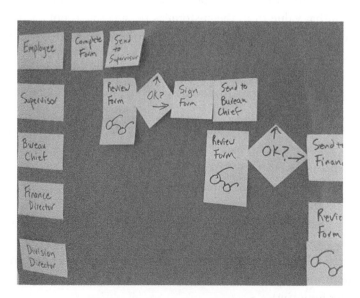

FIGURE 2.1

Map of an approval process using swim lanes for the process steps by different divisions within the organization.

- Arrange chairs and narrow table for team members in a "V" formation in front of the map, so they can converse easily with one another and all have access to the map.
- The facilitator identifies a team member to write step names and roles on sticky notes.
- In a column on the left side of the map, post a sticky note for each of the roles that touch the process (e.g. "receptionist," "accounts payable clerk," "team leader"). These "swim lanes" will illustrate the handoffs.
- Write the name of each step on a sticky note using a brief verb-noun format (e.g. "retrieve file," "complete requisition," "update report"). Either the facilitator or another team member places the steps on the map in the proper sequence.[6]
- The team members identify all steps and decision points executed within the current process.
- Team members work together to agree to a common understanding of the steps and the sequence, at least 80% of the time. Don't get distracted by examples of outliers, but note where work is nonstandard—where people in the same role do their work differently.
- Identify any existing documents that require the process to be conducted in a certain way.
- Identify major assumptions about the process and why things are done this way.

Mapping with Colors, Symbols, and Definitions

The map is a visual representation of the team's common understanding of the process. Mapping techniques vary among Lean practitioners. After trying to standardize the meaning of various colors and shapes of sticky notes, we've adopted a pragmatic view. Each team agrees on the meaning and uses the materials consistently. Our typical choices are:

- Steps—use a large rectangular sticky note for each step in the process. Use verb-noun format to describe the activity at that step. For example: "Receive application," "Send invoice," "Issue permit."
- Decision points—use square yellow sticky notes, pivoted to a diamond shape. Decision points can lead to alternative or parallel paths.
- "Bright ideas"—use either blue sticky notes, or draw a light bulb shape on a sticky note of any color. Post the ideas on a flip chart near

the process map to capture team members' suggestions. Often, teams are tempted to jump ahead to propose changes before they have finished documenting the current state. The "bright idea" system allows the team to stay focused on the task at hand, without losing the ideas.

- Monuments (obstacles to efficient operation)—use either a green sticky note or draw a monument on a sticky note of any color. Monuments are equipment or requirements that cannot be easily moved which interrupt the flow of work. In the manufacturing world, a monument may be a very large machine that is in the wrong place in the plant. It is not easily moved to a proper position. New Hampshire's Executive Council is an example of an operational monument. It is a level of government unique to the State, which could only be removed by amending the State's Constitution.

- Assumptions or questions—use an orange sticky note or draw a question mark on a sticky note of any color It can be useful when team members assume a process step is required. Employees often assume that departmental policies are required by law, but that may not be the case. Ask, "is it law or lore?" Not sure? Assign research. If step is required by statute, include the citation.

- *Kaizen* burst—draw sunburst on a large yellow sticky note. *Kaizen* burst is a supplemental project required to make this project successful, or a spin-off project that is related, but out of scope.

We encourage our teams to have fun while making the process visible. Graphics can be drawn on any color sticky note. Examples: Spectacles (inspection), paper clip (copies made), bottle (bottleneck), circle of arrows (rework), an unequal sign (nonstandard work). Teams can be creative to select graphics that convey visual meaning.

Calibration Meetings

Check-ins with the sponsor can occur, if appropriate. Typically, there is enough time in between scheduled work sessions for the PM or facilitator to update the sponsor. Some Lean practitioners prefer to wait until the project is completed and the entire team presents its work to the sponsor. Other practitioners schedule regular calibration meetings to assure that the team's direction is consistent with the sponsor's goals for the event. The facilitator might seek the sponsor's involvement to encourage the team, to reiterate the goals, or to approve changes to the charter. Input from the sponsor might be useful to the team in constructing the future state and the implementation plan. On the other hand, it is an empowering experience for the team to work independently until they are ready to present their completed work.

Metrics and Data Sheets

After the sequencing is completed for the current state, the team prepares data sheets on each step in the process. Various templates of data sheets can be used. A typical data sheet used in New Hampshire is below:

Step Number	Name/Description of Step
A. Work time—The actual work time to complete the task.	Typical: Min:　　Max:
B. Cycle time—The time it takes to complete the step: from the end of the previous step to the end of this step—including wait times, setup time, routing time, actual work time, and any delays.	Typical: Min:　　Max:
C. Accuracy vs. rework—The percentage of time the step is completed correctly the first time. (A low percentage means the work done at this step often requires rework.)	
Color coded assessments of value. Green = value added; red = non-valued added (*muda*); yellow = non-value added to the customer, but necessary to operate the business; orange = non-value added to the end-user customer, but value added to the public. (The use of orange is optional; it may be useful in mapping regulatory processes.)	

Alternatively, rather than using data sheets, some practitioners write the metrics directly on the sticky notes. Others use data sheets instead of sticky notes. Regardless of the mode, your team needs to know the amount of time it takes to do the work. Preparation for the project should include going to the *gemba* (the workplace) to observe flow and record data.

For the Yellow Belt class, participants are not required to bring a fully chartered project with documented metrics—it's their first introduction to the terminology and techniques. When a facilitator asks how long it takes to accomplish each step in the process, team members offer different estimates. Since the first Lean effort for most service processes could be expected to reduce the time by hours, days, or weeks, the facilitator asks the team not to get bogged down in debates about minutes. The data sheet template is constructed to allow a range of min–max and typical.

A data sheet is required for each step. Yellow Belt class project teams sometimes lack information about specific steps because the colleague who does that work is not enrolled in the class. This task illustrates why it's so important for the team to include the people who do the work.

Lean practitioners use different terminology for the two core measurements. The actual time it takes to preform each task may be called "work time," "process time," or "touch time." The elapsed time from the point the previous step is completed to the point the current step is completed may be called "cycle time," "lead time," or "turnaround time." The New Hampshire program uses the terms "work time" and "cycle time." The core concepts are the same.

The definitions of work time and cycle time are printed on the data sheets. The facilitator needs to reiterate the distinction as the group initially struggles with the task.

Instructions:

- Populate fields A and B for every step. If the team lacks specific data, rely on the members' estimates based on experience; avoid getting bogged down in debates about minutes.
- Use consistent increments of time for all steps (minutes and hours) to save time on analysis. Days should be counted as workdays; 7.5 or 8 hours, not 24. Weeks should be 5 days, not 7.
- The field C (accuracy) can be populated for every step to collect data about the quality of the entire process. Alternatively, it can be used selectively, only for the steps that require substantial rework. Example: If 60% of the applications for a permitting process are returned due to errors or incomplete information, the data sheet for the step "Prepare Application" would indicate a 40% accuracy rate.
- Note any special considerations. If the step is required by statute, provide the citation.
- Tape each of the sheets on the map—either attached to each sticky note or at the base of the map.

Patience is required because the task of analyzing a long-standing work process can be tedious. There may be tension within the group. The facilitator may need to remind the group that this project is not "extra" work; process improvement *is* your work. Each team member's input is valuable.

The development of a detailed understanding of the process provides the information necessary for comprehensive and meaningful improvements. And, the data sheet activity frequently uncovers steps that were overlooked in the initial mapping.

Value Assessment

After posting the data sheets and tracing the process path, the team evaluates the value of each step to the end-user customer. A colorful dot is placed on each data sheet based on the assessment of value.

- Green = The step adds value to the end-user customer by transforming materials or information into products or services the customer wants. It is done right the first time, and the customer is willing to pay for it.
- Yellow = The step does not add value to the customer but is essential to the operation of the organization. It is required for a valid reason.
- Red = The step adds no value to the customer or to the organization. It is *muda*.
- Orange can be used to signify value to the public. This is an optional category, which can be used to evaluate steps in regulatory processes. It is discussed in detail in Chapter 9.

Valuable employees; non-value-added work: As the team evaluates each step as Green, Red, or Yellow, the facilitator must remind the members that this is not a value judgment of the employees responsible for conducting the process. It's about the process. Absent this context, it can be extremely demoralizing to have your colleagues label your work as *muda*. Team members who have been assigned to do non-value-added work in the current process can be freed up for higher value-added work, increasing staff morale as well as organizational effectiveness. It may be useful to do some brainstorming about the potential use of the freed capacity and seek input from the sponsor. Quite likely, the sponsor has a long wish list of tasks.

Summary Table

Consistent with the goal of making things visible, the team tallies the metrics for the current state on flip chart paper.

	Current State	Future State	% Change
Total work time (typical)			
Total cycle time (typical)			
Total # steps			
• Value-added to the customer			
• Non-valued added			
• Non-value added—necessary			

Once the future state is designed and measured, complete the table and calculate the percentage of expected change. Bear in mind that it's not just about speed, but it's about value to the customer. Even if the total number of steps is not reduced, the redesign might gain quality by increasing the value-added steps, while decreasing the non-value added. Your summary table tells part of the story, but it's not the whole story. The next section describes these considerations.

Responsibility to Ask, "Why?"

Some processes have evolved over time in a way that was never documented. Others may have gone unexamined for so long that conditions may have evolved to contain redundancies or obsolete steps that no longer add value. A simple examination of such processes may result in immediate identification of improvement opportunities at little or no cost.

The "5 Whys" is a Lean method used to explore the cause/effect relationships underlying a problem. Why do we do the things we do? Ask "why" five times to understand the value of doing any step in a process. Lean teams often gain insights from the answers, and how seldom the answer is "because customers value the activity." The most common answer is "because that's the way it's always been done!" A sample of a "5 Whys" worksheet is provided in Chapter 8.

Designing and Mapping the Future State

As the team develops the new workflow, they move from "review, rework, redo" to "responsibility for quality." Deming's third point is "Cease dependence on inspection to achieve quality."[7]

Design for value, quality, and efficiency. A good process should produce reliable results each time the work is performed. The design should include judicious and strategic QCs within the process, not after the fact. Good process design minimizes errors. Avoid (or minimize) the checking of people's work. Use clear and concise instruction, and whenever possible use visual and/or auditory cues to avoid errors.

- Fail-safe controls: an error stops the line.
- Visual and/or audible controls as signals when a deviation occurs. For example: computer beeps, flashed messages asking the user, "Are you sure you want to delete?" or a reminder to attach a file to an email containing the word "attach."
- Checklists are particularly valuable for complex tasks with frequent repetition. Examples: processes used by medical personnel or airline flight crews.

Don't build the process for outliers. Process design built for exceptions will be unnecessarily complex. Lean seeks standard work. Design a process that will better serve customers, eliminate waste, and reduce cycle time. Envision the ideal process first. There will be time later to figure out what can be done immediately, what can be phased in, and what is not practical or feasible.

Move the current state map up on the wall. Tape another long piece of paper below it, so the team is able to see the current state map while they work on the future state.

Before mapping, check in with all bright ideas and assumptions. Encourage critical thinking and creativity, but avoid getting sidetracked.

Map the future state by writing new sticky notes for all the steps that will be retained while omitting those that will be eliminated. Some improvements may occur by re-sequencing existing steps to improve flow. Cycle time may be significantly improved due to a reduction in handoffs. Sometimes quality can be improved by adding a step. For example, requiring the use of a checklist could improve quality by standardizing the work and reducing errors.

Identify ideas that require further analysis to determine feasibility and cost/benefit impact. Mark these ideas as "*kaizen* bursts" to signify the potential for a spin-off project.

Once the future state map is completed, develop a data sheet based on best estimates for the work time and cycle time for each step. Post the results on your summary table.

Implementation Plan

Identify what needs to be done to make the future state a reality. Post the tasks on an impact-effort grid to indicate the degree of value and difficulty. Examples: developing a new data base may be "hard to do/big improvement"; posting a user-friendly checklist on a website may be "easy to do/ big improvement." The grid helps the team to prioritize its proposals. There is an example below:

Easy to do; big improvement	**Hard to do; big improvement**
Update the checklist on the web	Automate the enrollment process
Easy to do; small improvement	**Hard to do; small improvement**
Post the daily staff schedule	(avoid this category)

Next, prepare a detailed plan breaking down the tasks required to accomplish each of the changes. Focus first on no-cost and low-cost improvements. Include delivery timeframes and milestones necessary to ensure project implementation. Each item in the plan indicates who is accountable for delivery, and the resources required. Each item includes a start date, estimated duration of the task, and an end date. An example is below:

Task	Person(s) Responsible	Start/End Dates	Resource Needs	Deliverable(s)
Update checklist	Sally	June 1–June 21	Info from Roger	New checklist
Post checklist to website	Bob	June 21–June 22	Document from Sally	Web posting
Post the daily staff schedule	Sally	June 1– ongoing	none	Daily posting
Design an auto- enrollment option	Marge & IT team	June 1– September 1	IT support	Test sample
Roll out auto-enrollment	Marge & IT team	September 1–December 1	IT support	Go live

The Lean team should consider the potential resistance to the new process within the organization and develop strategies to reduce and overcome resistance to the new process. A good communication plan can make a big difference.

Communication Plan

The Lean team's communication plan guides them in sharing information on the status of project activities and critical dependencies to ensure success. It should contain mechanisms for customers and stakeholders to provide feedback to the team and to project management. The plan needs to consider how employees will learn about the new workflow.

The team determines how best to inform their colleagues about the planned changes, being mindful of how it will impact the work of those who have not been part of the team. The team plans the rollout, both in content and in timing. Some teams conduct workplace briefings while the project is going on. Others decide to wait until the project is completed and the sponsor has authorized the changes. They may adopt a multifaceted plan with one-on-one meetings, and a formal presentation by the team during a staff meeting.

Do they expect resistance, and if so, how should it be addressed? Avoid becoming defensive when questioned by colleagues. The team might have overlooked a factor that will lead to unintended negative consequences. Don't mistake sincere reservations with obstructionist behavior. On the other hand, some Lean projects never get off the ground due to inertia or outright sabotage from middle managers or others who oppose the changes. Consider the reasons for the resistance, and address it accordingly.

Once implemented, the future state becomes the new process. However, without a concerted effort, people may fall back into old habits or patterns. Look for opportunities to recognize and formally celebrate the gains publicly at each stage. In addition to sustaining the gains, these celebrations are opportunities to affirm Lean culture and encourage people to identify future projects.

Preparing the A3 Report

An A3 template is a Lean tool that covers the Plan–Do–Check–Act/Adjust (PDCA) cycle of continuous improvement on a single sheet of paper. The name "A3" refers to the 11″×17″ size of paper, but an A3 format can be used on any size of paper. Some teams use a poster board to display their A3 project summaries.

Project teams can use the template to prepare a concise report for the sponsor. The A3 typically has seven fields: Background, Current

Conditions, Management Goals, Root Cause Analysis, Countermeasures, Plan, and Follow-Up/Sustainment.

A sample A3 report is in Chapter 8.

"The Sell"—Lean Team Report to the Sponsor

It is rare for a sponsor to delegate complete authority to the project team; most will reserve judgment until the team completes its work. The team presents its work in a "sell"—a pitch to the sponsor to authorize the changes. Typically, the sponsor is supportive of the team's recommendations but may have questions or concerns about the organization's capacity to make rapid or significant changes.

The sell can take different forms depending upon the relationship of the sponsor to the team and the level of authority that has been delegated, and if the team has provided updates during the project.

Each team member should have a role in the presentation. The member speaking first should make it clear that the team does not expect a yes or no response on the spot. Essentially, the team walks the sponsor through the current state findings and explains the rationale for the proposed future state. The sponsor may consider the work unit's capacity to complete the tasks required by the implementation plan. A phased or modified implementation could be discussed.

Most sponsors need some time to consider the plan before authorizing the proposed changes. For example, sponsors of Lean projects at the Department of Safety commit to a response on the entire package within two weeks, although they might authorize portions of the proposal at the sell. Once the sponsor signs off on the plan, implementation goes forward. As the Lean program matures, sponsors and team members will get accustomed to using the sell as an opportunity for dialogue, followed by action.

Project Implementation

Prior to the close of the project, the team commits to a series of checkpoints—typically on a 30/60/90-day schedule. These progress updates should identify all tasks, noting which are completed, pending, or behind schedule. Barriers must be identified and countermeasures developed. The team keeps the sponsor informed of the progress, and seeks assistance in the removal of obstacles, if necessary.

A proactive sponsor plays a role in communicating the new expectations to staff, customers, and stakeholders. The sponsor's involvement serves multiple purposes—to assure the project's success, to express commitment to the Lean initiative, and to build a culture of continuous improvement.

Don't underestimate the time and attention required for the follow-through. Many early Lean projects fail at the implementation stage. Lean team members are so enthusiastic that they assume that the changes will be made. The visual proof provided by the maps speaks for itself, right? We've all agreed to proceed, right? Of course, the new way of doing business will start immediately. Maybe not.

Lean projects can go off the rails in several ways. First, the team returns to a pile of work that has built up while they were in the Lean event, so they may lose track of the tasks needed to make the transition. Second, lacking clarity about the role of the team leader/PM, the Lean facilitator and the agency's Lean coordinator can leave the ball on the ground in the middle of the field. Third, many Lean practitioners are only belatedly coming to grips with the range of skills required to be a successful PM. Lean practitioners are increasingly being trained in PM concepts and skills.

In most models, the team leader is responsible for tracking of the implementation plan. In some organizations, the Lean facilitator or Lean coordinator may also be involved in follow-up activities. For example, DHHS has initiated "wrap-around services" whereby one of the department's Lean coordinators works with a team post-event through implementation. (This model will be discussed in more detail in Chapter 10.) Regardless of the model selected, attention to detail at this stage is critical. *Kaizen* events without implementation are *muda*.

Use the Lean concept of visual management to keep everyone informed of the progress. Post the plan on a wall and/or electronically in a shared drive and accessible to all team members and business managers affected by the process changes. Follow the communication plan to ensure that stakeholders, management, and team members receive timely status reports.

The 30/60/90-day check-ins can be electronic. However, the team might also meet with the sponsor periodically to confirm that the deliverables are on target, and to celebrate significant milestones.

Be sure to add a feedback system—the PDCA cycle requires improvements to be tested, validated, and sustained. Determine how outcomes of the new process will be measured, and the mechanisms for the project team and stakeholders to provide feedback to project management.

MOVING FORWARD WITH LEAN AFTER COMPLETING THE YELLOW BELT PROGRAM

Instructions to the trainer: Design class follow-ups after 6 and 12 months. Ask each team to send project status updates to the YB class instructor, so they can be posted on the Lean website, with photos of each team. Provide contact information for agency Lean coordinators and Lean facilitators.

Instructions to participants:

- Stay in touch with the class project team as the project goes forward and follow through on any implementation tasks assigned to you.
- Inform your agency's Lean coordinator of your Yellow Belt certificate and any suggestions you have for more *kaizen* projects.
- If your agency doesn't have an active Lean program, seek colleagues who share your interest in process improvement to consider the best way to get started. Solicit ideas for projects and organize teams to go to training, or to arrange an onsite project. Experienced Lean facilitators may be available to work with a team onsite.

Summary: Lean is associated with tools for mapping business processes, identifying improvement, and charting progress. Lean is also an attitude and philosophy about continuous improvement, maximizing the value for customers and citizens. While perfection is unobtainable, the Lean organization is always seeking ways to do things better and continuous change becomes part of the culture.

The Food Bank *Kaizen* clip posted on YouTube is less than 7 minutes long, and it is an inspiring look at how Lean practitioners from Toyota worked with a local food bank in New York City. "Meals Per Hour" is a delightful way to show service sector workers how Lean applies to us.[8]

SUMMARY OF LESSONS LEARNED

Training is an integration of presentation and application. The multilevel program integrates concepts and tools with hands-on skill practices.

The Yellow Belt training builds capacity for the Lean initiative by

- Completing real projects,

- Providing practice opportunities to build the skills of Lean facilitators,
- Generating an increasing cadre of trained staff who will be enthusiastic participants.

APPLYING THE LESSONS

- The training unit needs to work with agency Lean coordinators to prepare a steady strea m of real projects for Ye llow Belt classes. If the agency has a priority project of appropriate scope for the 3-day session, the selection of the project determines the participants. For a successful project, the team must include the people who do the work. Participants registering without a team will join one of the projects as fresh eyes.
- Agency leadership should identify staff who will be expected to join the ranks of the Lean change agents to send to Yellow Belt training, and beyond. Recall that Commissioner Barthelmes selected Chris and Roberta to attend the first training session.
- The training unit needs an ample supply of Green Belts to work with the project teams during Yellow Belt classes. Management must support the time of these facilitators to work with project teams during the training.
- Since Lean is an essential field of knowledge for supervisors and managers, include the Yellow Belt class in the Certified Public Supervisor (CPS) program. Starting in 2018, all CPS students in New Hampshire will graduate from the program with a Yellow Belt.
- Build the cadre: As participants receive Yellow Belt certificates, add them to a growing e-mail distribution list. Use the list to send notices of upcoming events, links to the website, and invitations to follow the blog.

NOTES

1 "Lean in Government Starter Kit," Environmental Protection Agency. Accessed February 22, 2018 v.4.0 September 2017 expands upon the original Starter Kit. www.epa.gov/lean/lean-government-starter-kit-version-40.

2 "Dr. Deming's 14 Points for Management," The Deming Institute. Accessed February 13, 2018. https://deming.org/explore/fourteen-points.

3 "Dr. Deming's 14 Points for Management," The Deming Institute. Accessed February 13, 2018. https://deming.org/explore/fourteen-points.

4 "Introduction to Lean Thinking," State of Washington. Accessed February 22, 2018. www.youtube.com/watch?v=RxDw0Q_gVt0.

5 The W. Edwards Deming Institute. W. Edwards Deming Quotes. Accessed August 7, 2018. http://quotes.deming.org/quote/10091.

6 Sam McKeeman recommended that the team start with the last step and work backward to the beginning of the process. To use this method, start on the right side of the paper and move toward the left. Sam explained that it would use a different part of the brain. This is quite challenging, and we haven't made it standard practice— our teams typically start with the first step in the process and work to the end.

7 "Dr. Deming's 14 Points for Management," The Deming Institute. Accessed February 13, 2018. https://deming.org/explore/fourteen-points.

8 Video "Meals Per Hour" Written by Jeff Gonic. Directed by Henry Joost and Ariel Shulman. Supermarche, June 19, 2013. Accessed April 19, 2018. www.youtube.com/watch?v=EedMmMedj3M.

3

You're the Night Shift

Chapter 3's title is a comment made by Jim Womack to our team of Lean activists over a beer in 2013, and therein lies a tale.

Emboldened by our successful first summit, we set our sights high for 2013. Lean Executive Committee member Liz Gray contacted the Lean Enterprise Institute and invited Jim Womack to be keynote speaker. We couldn't believe our good fortune when the coauthor of *The Machine That Changed the World* not only agreed to speak at the summit, but asked to meet with our Lean team a month in advance of the event to hear about our work.

We set an agenda for "Jim Womack Day" and prepared a series of presentations to show off our projects. As a true Lean groupie, I asked him to sign my copy of *The Machine*. Our Lean leaders presented the maps of our most successful projects. We were somewhat crestfallen when Jim explained that maps were not the point—it was management. He spent time with us that day explaining that we needed to move from working on exceptions (like one-off projects) to continual change—continuously responding to new situations.

He brought copies of his book, *Gemba Walks*, for us and for our agency commissioners, with the key lesson, "Management is more important than tools."[1] Reminding us of the importance of going to the *gemba* (the real place, where value is made), he asked to take a "*gemba* walk" through our Division of Motor Vehicles (DMV). "No walk, no talk," he told us. Since the DMV was an early priority for process improvement for the Department, the DOS Lean team eagerly arranged a walk-through. Roberta later recalled that Jim knew that the escorted tour was too artificial to be a real *gemba* walk. We had a lot to learn. He encouraged us to read *Learning to See* by John Shook.

Jim returned the day before the summit to meet with agency commissioners, so he could explain the important role for leadership in Lean organizations. He encouraged the leaders of the five largest agencies to apply Lean principles, redirecting line managers away from workarounds and firefighting, and toward engaging their people in process improvement. He stressed that the improvement team needs technical skills in Lean, which are not gained from books or lectures, but by experience. Top leadership plays a crucial role in the transformation by setting clear expectations. He reminded them that a primary concern for mid-level managers is "How do I avoid negative consequences?"

Following Jim's meeting with the commissioners, several of us had an opportunity to have a beer with him. Looking at our ragtag band of Lean activists, Jim observed, "You're the night shift." It took a moment for us to understand. He was letting us know that our Lean journey would be limited because we all had "day jobs" in our organizations—none of our job descriptions said we were assigned to Lean (Figure 3.1).

Dr. Womack's 2013 visit hit us on two levels. First, he taught us that it's not about the maps—it's about the management. Let's discuss these two subjects separately.

FIGURE 3.1
Jim Womack addressing the Lean summit (2013).

#1 LEAN = BROWN PAPER, AND COLORFUL STICKY NOTES ... OR DOES IT?

When Jim explained that maps aren't the point, it took us a while to understand that Lean isn't just about *kaizen* events. We knew that *kaizen* has the broader meaning of "change for the better," but we were unclear of how to apply the concept to a workforce accustomed to following rules. There was an apparent contradiction between standard work and continuous improvement. It would take much more studying to understand those concepts before applying them.

We started by expanding our knowledge of Lean tools. To adapt an adage: if the only tool you have is a process map, everything looks like a *kaizen* event.

In our enthusiasm to make process maps, we had overlooked some of the other Lean tools that were presented in Sam's original training. On a *gemba* walk to the DES offices, Sam explained how a visit to the worksite—the *gemba*—is critical to understanding how processes are really conducted. He also demonstrated the Spaghetti Diagram, a tool for tracing the flow of people and materials throughout the workplace to identify unnecessary motion, and explained how it can identify the optimal location of office equipment and machines or staff. He introduced the 5S using the English translations of Sort, Set in order, Shine, Standardize and Sustain. He encouraged us to apply it as part of our regular work. We relearned these lessons and more.

Lean practitioners with a background in business analytics or statistical analysis had a jump on those of us from other fields. They were already familiar with tools such as Pareto charts, affinity diagrams, fishbone diagrams, histograms, and scatter plots. Integration of these tools allowed *kaizen* events to drill down to root causes, prioritizing countermeasures of maximum impact.

We steadily expanded our understanding of Lean principles and techniques. The spirit of "just do it" was manifested in the early work at the DOT. Innovative DOT staff in maintenance sheds throughout the state conducted "tailgate lean"—creative improvements in their daily work.

Regardless of the tools used, the core lesson that "it's not about maps, it's about management" was still percolating. In *Government That Works*,

John Bernard suggested that the focus on events and tools was lean with a "little l", rather than as a management system (big "L"Lean).[2]

Subsequent chapters will delve into the challenge of integrating *kaizen* events into a broad culture of continuous improvement within a Lean organization.

#2 ROGUE ENERGY IS UNSUSTAINABLE. A LEAN INITIATIVE NEEDS INFRASTRUCTURE

We were "the night shift" because our primary duties (our "day jobs") were not as Lean practitioners or coordinators. Dr. Womack had put a name to it. Regardless of our enthusiasm for Lean, our capacity fluctuated with the demands of our regular duties. A sustainable Lean program would require staff assigned specifically to the initiative. But, despite evidence of private sector success with Lean, we knew not to get our hopes up.

Those of us who had worked for the state in 2008 remembered that the state's shortsighted management was documented in "Grading the States" by the Pew Research Center.[3] New Hampshire received the lowest ranking of any state, with a grade of D-plus.

The Pew report noted: "There is a myth that New Hampshire's fiscally conservative state culture creates frugal but fit government—no taxes, no frills, no problem. In truth, while New Hampshire may provide fewer services than other states, the notion that its finances are emblematic of old-fashioned New England Puritanism just isn't true. Meager cost and performance information and tortuous business processes create an institutional inertia that wastes much of the state's limited resources..."[4]

In 2009, a Lean program participant told Rep. Borden, "I worked for the government of Massachusetts for 19 years before I came to work in New Hampshire. The government of New Hampshire is much more bureaucratic. It is really hard to get anything done here and it's more expensive."[5]

Fast forward to 2014. Despite the successes touted at our Lean summits in 2012 and 2013, few of the statewide bureaucratic processes had changed since the Pew report's release in 2008. While both Governors John Lynch and Maggie Hassan were enthusiastic supporters of Lean, they were unable to persuade the New Hampshire Legislature to appropriate funds for an Office of Lean.

Governor Hassan's efforts were marked by her establishment of the Commission on Innovation, Efficiency, and Transparency in 2014. The commission was comprised of private sector and governmental leaders including three of the agency heads who had met with Jim Womack: Tom Burack (DES), Chris Clement (DOT), and Linda Hodgdon (DAS).

The commission's report, released in 2015, referenced the D-plus grade from Pew.[6] The report confirmed that many of the tortuous administrative processes for basic business functions were still in use. One particularly unLean example highlighted the fact that administrators had little flexibility to manage their agency budgets. Approval for any variation in the biennial budget's more than 12,000 line items, or permission to reclassify personnel added thousands of hours of administrative time. Other unLean examples included an annual physical count of as many as 60,000 items with a purchase price of less than $2,000. Such "monuments" impeded the ability of Lean teams to reduce time spent on wasteful tasks and to redeploy staff to higher value-added activities.

On the bright side, the report acknowledged significant gains in process improvement by several departments and credited the Lean work in those agencies. Several of the DOS, DES and DAS projects were described, as well as a DHHS project at the state's psychiatric hospital that reengineered their discharge program, reducing the 30-day readmission rates by 25%.

While praising those gains, the Commission understood that innovation could not be attained by sporadic efforts. They made a strong case for a sustained, systemic, strategic approach.

> New Hampshire State Government's record on innovation and efficiency is more a reflection of individual initiative and ad hoc efforts than an institutional commitment to the sort of informed transparency, management processes, and resource commitments that can permanently change the trajectory of the state's operating performance. As a consequence, state government operating performance lags its peers and the private sector. What the citizens of New Hampshire deserve and should require is not a few innovations, but state government that is innovative; not a set of efficiency efforts, but state government that drives efficiency constantly; and not a state government whose expenses only are transparent, but one whose

performance is transparent. Fortunately, there are ample opportunities for improvement...not just in a set of projects.... but in the operating management of the institution.[7]

Below are excerpts from the Commission's recommendations:

- The Executive Branch will reengineer 15% of Executive Branch processes annually with the target of reducing time and resources required for those processes by 20%.
- As a test case, using one of the Departments with a working Balanced Scorecard, map all current control processes...and develop a proposal to shift 20% of the time/resources currently devoted to controls to management and oversight of performance while meeting proper control obligations.
- The Executive Branch will devote at least 0.1% of operating expense and 5% of the capital budget to innovation efforts.

Governor Hassan's 2014–2015 budget proposed an Office of Government Innovation and Efficiency to implement the commission's recommendations. The office would work with agencies on Lean efforts, and a series of proactive initiatives. The proposed Innovation and Efficiency Fund would be augmented by savings from efficiency initiatives, and 20% percent of the savings from the efficiency gains would remain in the department that conducted the project.

The funding was not approved by the legislature.

According to *The Lean Toolbox*, a sustainable Lean initiative requires a Lean promotion office (LPO) or continuous improvement office comprising. 05%–2% of the workforce working as internal Lean consultants, depending on the phase of the initiative. "The ideal head of the LPO is a respected Lean believer, and an influential individual who works through line managers, helping them to achieve their Lean goals."[8]

Without a statewide mandate and adequate resources to train and deploy personnel, our Lean initiative grew in fits and starts, based on fluctuations in agency priorities and personnel changes. We were unable to tackle the most significant cross-agency *muda* that earned the D-plus grade.

Access to training was erratic. The Bureau of Education & Training (BET) lacked funding to provide the Lean training without charging the agencies, which excluded agencies without training funds. In contrast,

Vermont's Lean program includes broad access to training. When Vermont's Lean coordinator, Justin Kenney, was asked by one of our New Hampshire Lean practitioners how much their classes cost, he simply replied, "I do the training." New Hampshire's cost barrier has been a source of *muri* and discouragement for those of us who were eager to get a movement going.

Even agencies with funding were so overwhelmed by the *muri* of chronic staff shortages, managers couldn't image taking the time to send staff to Lean training.

The next several chapters describe our creative workarounds—which may be instructive. In the meantime, it's not all bad news for our ragtag group of true believers.

Due to the commitment of leading commissioners, valuable projects continued at the agency level. Notably, several commissioners assigned staff members to shepherd Lean efforts in their agencies. DOS Assistant Commissioner Kevin O'Brien provided leadership that was critical to the success of Lean coordinators Roberta Witham and Chris Wagner, including saving nearly $250,000 in returned mail costs and updating the process for criminal background checks. Commissioner Nick Toumpas (DHHS) assigned the Quality Improvement Office's John MacPhee to lean processes for the state's psychiatric hospital and the disability determination unit. Both projects improved the quality of service, while reducing costs.

DES Commissioner Tom Burack assigned Bob Minicucci, one of the environmental engineers on his staff, to do Lean work as part of his regular job. Tom also approved the use of Bob's time to facilitate the cross-agency affiliation of Lean practitioners. Bob became the chair of the fledgling NH Lean Executive Committee.

FROM A SUPPORT GROUP TO A COMMUNITY OF PRACTICE

When a dozen practitioners from various agencies convened as a Lean Network, meetings were essentially round robins of storytelling. We each took turns sharing the accounts of our agency Lean efforts. When anyone mentioned an obstacle, the others in the group chimed in with advice. It was supportive and encouraging.

Several agencies with supportive commissioners authorized staff to participate in the Lean Network and to work on Lean projects. While most of the agency Lean representatives still had other job duties, their managers trusted them to balance those duties appropriately. This practice was consistent with the Lean principle of trusting employees and aligning authority and responsibility at the lowest possible level. Network participation fluctuated somewhat based on the demands of the "day jobs" of various members, but the core group became increasingly cohesive.

The Lean Network continued to meet and gradually transformed from an informal support group to an intentional community of practice. Meanwhile, the Lean coordinators from each agency formed a leadership team, which became the Lean Executive Committee (LEC). While Network meetings continued to be open to all who shared our interested in Lean, the LEC was intended to have a strategic role. One of the driving forces in the transformation was Major Michael Moranti, who joined the network as a representative of the New Hampshire Army National Guard. The major's training in tactical and strategic leadership, along with his access to staff resources, made him a valuable member.

During June and July of 2013, Major Moranti facilitated strategic planning sessions for LEC. The group agreed on a mission: "In order to promote a stronger and more efficient New Hampshire, the LEC will facilitate innovation and effectiveness for all state agencies and their partners through Lean process improvement."

Excerpts from LEC's SWOT analysis follow:

- Strengths: expertise in state government, experience in Lean, collaboration and communication channels, established and dedicated people.
- Weaknesses: no state mandate, no funding, quasi-organization, varied Lean practices based on organizational culture, no succession plan, difficult to organize cross-silo projects and teams to get maximum benefits, lack of overall direction and coordination (optimization).
- Opportunities: varied experience, program simplicity (Lean is applicable at all levels), we can change how government services are delivered.

FIGURE 3.2
Pictured: Linda Hodgdon (then Commissioner of Administrative Services), Rep. David Borden, Kevin O'Brien (then Chief of Policy and Planning for the Department of Safety), Kate McGovern (then Associate Professor, Bureau of Education &Training).

- Threats: time, money, staff called to focus on other duties, political movement to "shrink government," view of Lean as "flavor of the month/year," and department culture dictates

Among the primary goals were to increase organizational legitimacy and acknowledgement by developing a charter, a structure, roles, and a succession plan. LEC members also agreed to strive for a cross-functional big win, to develop performance measures and training standards, and to educate stakeholders on the value of Lean.

While still striving to share best practices among agencies and plan the agendas for the Network meetings, the LEC also functioned as a planning committee for the first two Lean summits (2012, 2013). During the 2013 summit, we recognized Representative David Borden for his role in starting our movement (Figure 3.2).

These two summits, with the support of sitting governors, drew hundreds of participants and generated much enthusiasm, and the recognition buoyed our spirits. However, event planning by committee was labor intensive and inefficient—lots of *muda*. It was difficult enough to balance our "day jobs" with our *kaizen* projects. Coordinating a major public event took time and effort away from the improvement work. Lacking the resources for proper event management, we opted not to try for a third summit in 2014 when the proposed Office of Lean was again defeated by the legislature. The weaknesses and threats of no money and no coordination prevailed.

Despite the continued gaps at the statewide level, we gained a significant resource in our training unit in late 2013. Major Moranti retired from the Guard and took a position as a Lean trainer for BET. While I continued to provide Yellow Belt training, he restructured the Continuous Improvement Practitioner certificate into a Green Belt program and initiated the first Black Belt program in 2015. Although access to training was still skewed by funding limitations, the cadre of Lean practitioners grew and continued to expand in depth and capacity. Five of the LEC members enrolled in the first Black Belt program, along with ten other committed Lean practitioners.

Persistent lack of funding for the training unit resulted in yet another setback. Michael Moranti left the temporary position in BET just as his first class of Black Belts graduated. Overwhelmed by the *muri*, I left for a premature retirement. I later returned part-time and restarted the program with the assistance of several of the Black Belt/ LEC members who served as guest faculty and mentors for subsequent Black Belt students. The cohesion and commitment kept the program going.

Throughout the strategic planning sessions and the Black Belt program, Michael had argued that a sustainable Lean program can't be "personality dependent." It should be able to survive the departure of any individual. Here's where *mura* (unevenness) comes into play. There was no plan for continuity to address personnel turnover. The weaknesses and threats identified by LEC continued to impact the initiative.

Lean coordinators would be absent from the LEC meetings and be unable to do any Lean projects for months at a time, due to the demands of their "day jobs." When a "night shift" Lean coordinator left an agency, there was no real job description to fill. Lean programs in the departments of Employment Security, Corrections, Agriculture, Labor, Administrative Services, and Resources and Economic Development stalled for significant periods due to staff or management turnover.

The cross-functional big win that LEC had hoped to achieve was also derailed. We conducted two Lean events to adopt an online learning platform, but we failed to implement as planned. The details will be discussed in Chapter 5, "How to Get Away with *Muda*."

Despite the setbacks, the hardy core of Lean practitioners persisted, supported by several key Commissioners. Thanks to their leadership and our initiative, we achieved our LEC goal of a signed charter. In August of 2015, the State Lean Network Executive Committee Charter was signed by 16 commissioners, giving an official endorsement to what had previously been a self-defined organization. The LEC's role was defined as providing "structure, guidance, and oversight for the overarching State Lean Network," and it recognized the network as being comprised of "Lean-trained members working to improve business processes using Lean tools at state agencies, municipalities, and non-profits that work with government bodies."

AGENCY LEAN COORDINATORS

We designed a job description for a Lean coordinator—even though it's not officially recognized in the State's job classification system. Since it's not official, Lean coordinators aspire to conduct these duties, in addition to those on their actual job descriptions.

Overview of Lean Coordinator's Duties
Leads the planning, facilitation, and management of Lean process improvement projects to meet the agency's strategic and operational goals. Serves as the organization's primary point of contact and coordination for all Lean activities. Participates in the Lean statewide network for the advancement of Lean standards, training, and promotion of a Lean culture within state government and private sector organizations. Directs project teams and resources within the agency. Fosters mentoring and training opportunities for Lean facilitators and Lean champions. Acts as a change agent for the deployment of process improvement initiatives. Presents regular updates, intended future plans, and models to senior management. Directs and tracks the work of the Lean Continuous Improvement Practitioners.

Key Responsibilities

- Manages small- and large-scale, agency-wide process improvement projects to meet business objectives, while delivering the highest levels of quality solutions, innovation, operational performance and customer satisfaction.
- Leads efforts to continually improve practices by adding quality and value while identifying and eliminating unnecessary or redundant steps.
- Maintains and manages the master list of all process improvement initiatives within the agency.
- Evaluates, prioritizes, and resources Lean projects.
- Responsible for implementing an effective method for continually communicating the status and results of improvement efforts throughout the organization.
- Presents project plans, future state models, potential barriers, and solutions to managers and senior management.
- Formulates improvement opportunities/proposals into project charters and work plans.
- Establishes and manages cross-functional teams consisting of internal and external stakeholders.
- Manages multiple projects simultaneously.
- Assists in the development and deployment of Lean training programs for all levels of management and the work force.
- Is responsible for leading and creating, with senior management support, a Lean culture within the agency.
- Works with the State Lean Network to develop standards provide enrichment and leverage solutions, and promote a Lean culture within state government and member organizations.
- Provides comprehensive Lean expertise, consultation, modeling, support, and professional presentations.
- Stays current with industry-wide advances in Lean standards and trends to continually leverage the best Lean practices and tools within the agency.
- Continuously works to recruit and mentor individuals with demonstrated exemplary interpersonal, listening, and problem-solving skills to build Lean capacity within the agency.
- Works collaboratively with agency staff to empower employees and draw groups to consensus.

The Lean Coordinator supports the community of practice through attending and participating in:

1. Monthly Lean Executive Committee meetings
2. Quarterly Lean Network meetings
3. Guest-speaking to support Bureau of Education and Training's Lean programs
4. Mentoring Lean Green Belt/Black Belt students for projects and general support
5. Other training or invited opportunities for professional growth and development.

When agency Lean coordinators were able to balance their other duties with this aspirational role, they did some terrific work. The Lean effort gained maturity in form and function. The Lean Network continued as an open community of practice, with the LEC serving as a guiding leadership body. With the functions bifurcated, the network served to welcome new participants including nonprofit organizations and the university system, providing programmatic instruction and networking opportunities. The LEC aspired to reach into the strategic possibilities for Lean.

SUMMARY OF LESSONS LEARNED

<u>Lesson 1:</u> It's not about the maps; it's about the management.
As explained by the Shingo Institute:

"Organizations can never sufficiently release the full potential of their people by creating a tool-oriented culture."[9] *The Lean Handbook* defines a lean culture as "the sum total of all the lean tools, techniques, and knowledge that exist within an organization at the root level and that fuel the overall organization alignment via collective lean thoughts, words, and actions toward the elimination of waste and the creation of value."[10]

In *Lean for the Public Sector*, Bert Teeuwen reminds us, "It is of the utmost importance not to consider Lean as a set of smart tools that improve processes or cut back costs. Lean is a way of thinking, an attitude."[11] In a discussion about the big picture, former DES Commissioner Tom Burack recommended the book *Government that Works* by John

M. Bernard.[12] As we discussed the use of Lean at a strategic rather than tactical level, Tom recalled, "that was what Jim Womack was trying to explain to us."

Lesson 2: A sustainable Lean initiative requires resources. Training must be made available. Staff at all levels in the organization needs to have the time to attend training and to participate in *kaizen* events. Advanced training needs to be available for staff that will be assigned as Lean facilitators and coordinators. These roles should be a core part of their jobs, not an ad-hoc add-on. As Deming's point #13 said, "Institute a vigorous program of education and self-improvement."[13]

Lesson 3: Ad-hoc efforts cannot reach the strategic level. While committed Lean practitioners will find a way to integrate Lean into their daily work, they lack the clout or the reach to grow the effort. *Kaizen* will remain a tactical tool, failing to transform the organization. If enough of the "night shift" gives up and moves on, the Lean initiative will most likely wither away.

Within 4 years of Jim Womack's meeting with the five leading commissioners (DES, DOS, DHHS, DAS and DOT), only one (DOS) remained in his position. The new commissioners didn't know about LEC—their predecessors had signed our charter. To address this gap, we developed a Lean for Leaders program, which is described in Chapter 7.

APPLYING THE LESSONS

- Initiating a Lean program requires support from top administrators. Those Lean champions should seek change agents who will form a cadre of early adopters, while assuring adequate resources for training.
- It's great to be praised by top management as they recognize the value of *kaizen* projects. Such encouragement boosts the morale of fledgling Lean practitioners—but that alone is not enough.
- The energy and enthusiasm of early adopters should be organized into a cross-silo steering committee, officially recognized with a charter. That organization should be a vehicle to connect the efforts of Lean practitioners to leadership's strategic goals. It can become a symbiosis—operating both top-down and bottom up.

Challenge: Without the broader context about Lean management, how will leaders know that it's not just about the maps?

In the ensuing chapters, we'll continue to explore the path through the *muri* as we moved forward. We'll also look at some states with successful Lean initiatives that came from the top. But since such important energy for our program came from the Lean practitioners, we'll move first to an overview of the Green Belt program.

NOTES

1 Jim Womack, *Gemba Walks* (The Lean Enterprise Institute, Cambridge, 2011) 312.
2 John M. Bernard, *Government That Works: The Results Revolution in the States* (Results America, Thompson Shore, 2015) 224.
3 Katherine Barrett and Richard Greene, "Grading the States: A Management Report Card," Pew Charitable Trusts, Governing Magazine (March 2008). Accessed February 22, 2018. www.pewtrusts.org/~/media/legacy/uploadedfiles/pcs_assets/2008/gradingthestates2008pdf.pdf.
4 Katherine Barrett and Richard Greene, "Grading the States: A Management Report Card," Pew Charitable Trusts, Governing Magazine (March 2008) (70). Accessed February 22, 2018. www.pewtrusts.org/~/media/legacy/uploadedfiles/pcs_assets/2008/gradingthestates2008pdf.pdf70.
5 David Borden, "What is Lean Government?" (October 22, 2009, Unpublished).
6 "Report of the Governor's Commission on Innovation, Efficiency, and Transparency," Submitted to Governor Maggie Hassan on January 19, 2015. Accessed February 13, 2018. www.innovations.harvard.edu/sites/default/files/opex/documents/Report%20of%20the%20Governor%27s%20Commission%20on%20Innovation%2C%20Efficiency%2C%20and%20Transparency%2C%20New%20Hampshire%2C%202015.pdf.
7 "Report of the Governor's Commission on Innovation, Efficiency, and Transparency," Submitted to Governor Maggie Hassan on January 19, 2015 (2). Accessed February 13, 2018. www.innovations.harvard.edu/sites/default/files/opex/documents/Report%20of%20the%20Governor%27s%20Commission%20on%20Innovation%2C%20Efficiency%2C%20and%20Transparency%2C%20New%20Hampshire%2C%202015.pdf.
8 John Bicheno and Matthias Holweg, *The Lean Toolbox 5th Edition* (Picsie Books, 2016) 73.
9 "The Shingo Model for Operational Excellence," The Shingo Institute, p. 13.
10 Anthony Manos and Chad Vincent, Editors, *The Lean Handbook* (ASQ Quality Press, Milwaukee, WI, 2012) 2.
11 Bert Teeuwen, *Lean for the Public Sector: The Pursuit of Perfection in Public Service* (Taylor& Francis Group, LLC, Productivity Press, New York, 2011) xii.
12 John M. Bernard, *Government That Works: The Results Revolution in the States* (Results America, Thompson Shore, 2015).
13 "Dr. Deming's 14 Points for Management," The Deming Institute. Accessed February 13, 2018. https://deming.org/explore/fourteen-points.

4

Go for the Green Belt

This chapter summarizes the Lean Green Belt program provided by the NH Bureau of Education & Training. The program is primarily focused on training Lean project facilitators, although some participants take the program to gain a better understanding of techniques and principles to prepare for supporting Lean initiatives in other roles. The chapter begins with an overview of the program, followed by a summary of the four modules, and closes with applications for lessons learned.

GREEN BELT PROGRAM

Green Belts (GBs) are change agents who lead and support efforts to improve the effectiveness and efficiency of an organization. They facilitate teams to identify and implement changes in the operation aimed at reducing waste, cost, time, and variation while increasing customer satisfaction. GBs apply these tools as part of their daily work and in specific improvement initiatives.

Learning objectives of the Green Belt program:

- Acquire facilitation skills and develop insight into group dynamics
- Use Lean tools including process mapping, A3, 5S, 5 Whys and practice facilitating a *kaizen* event
- Apply change management principles to Lean, as an organizational management system
- Plan to take a role in furthering Lean initiatives in your organization

Program Requirements

- Classes: Complete the 3-day program and related assignments and find a mentor.
- Practicum:
    - Facilitate or co-facilitate a project team during a Yellow Belt class or at another *kaizen*
    - Conduct an After-Action Review (AAR) with your mentor: what went well; what went not so well? Summarize lessons learned.
    - Prepare an A3 report on the project and send it to your project team, the agency's Lean coordinator, and BET Lean faculty.
- Maintaining active status as a Green Belt:
    - Continue to facilitate projects, use other Lean tools, and submit A3 project reports.
    - Seek additional learning about Lean independently, and with your mentor. Attend at least one continuing education workshop or Lean Network event each year.
    - Prepare an annual A3 report on a project you facilitated during that year. Send it to your mentor, your agency's Lean coordinator and to BET Lean faculty.

Pre-assignment: Recall the *kaizen* project team in your Yellow Belt class, or another Lean project in which you were a participant. What worked well? Not so well? What would you have done differently if you had been the facilitator? Was the project implemented? Why or why not? Were there any improvements in efficiency or effectiveness?

_____

CLASS TOPICS

Day 1
- Introduction to the program and discussion of pre-assignment and goals
- Facilitation skills, group dynamics, personality types
- Stages of team formation, brainstorming, and decision making
- Self-assessment as a facilitator
- Review of basic components of a *kaizen* event

- Facilitation practice—Part 1. Using a hypothetical project, participants take turns leading the initial phases of a *kaizen* event—ground rules, charter, and current state mapping.

Day 2
- Overview of Lean Management
- *Gemba* walks and 5S
- Tactical topics: resistance to change and barriers to implementation
- Lean tools for root cause analysis
- The A3 for project documentation and problem-solving
- Facilitation practice—Part 2. Continuing with the hypothetical project, participants take turns leading the next phases of a *kaizen* event—metrics & data sheets, future state mapping, the summary sheet, and an implementation plan.

Day 3
- The role of Lean teams and how Lean practitioners need to connect project work with strategic goals. Assessment of organizational readiness.
- Table discussion topics
- Facilitation practice—Part 3. Continuing with the hypothetical project, participants take turns leading the concluding phases of a *kaizen* event. Complete an A3 report on the project, including a sustainment plan, and present a sell to the hypothetical sponsor.
- Completing your Green Belt practicum and requirements to maintain active status
- Closing and evaluation

OVERVIEW OF THE PROGRAM

The material is divided into four modules, each dealing with a separate set of skills and concepts. A module on facilitation skills is followed by specific instructions for facilitating *kaizen* events. A module on change management and Lean management precedes a module on Lean tools.

Introduction: A Lean facilitator is responsible for leading a group of knowledgeable people, drawing out points of view, and bringing them to a consensus decision point. Aside from the direct gains in quality, productivity, and efficiency, the project provides a secondary gain of improved organizational communication and cohesion. Group activity in continuous improvement tends to:

- Build group ownership. A process is not one person's work, but the organization's. As participants become involved across units, a culture of continuous improvement becomes a norm for the organization. It exemplifies the Lean principle of workforce responsibility for operational excellence.
- Gain awareness of the data and, therefore, of the process itself. Lean events are designed to get agreement on process structure. Facilitated resolution helps the group understand the need for metrics.
- Standardize best practices. The event reveals differences among people performing the same steps, exposing the group to different ways of doing their work. The group designs the new standard workflow based on value to the customer.
- Derive consensus on changes to make to the process. Rather than impose changes from management or from outside the process, those involved in the process drive the change and, as a result, own it and its outcome.
- Build buy-in to the change process and build process ownership. As the groups incorporate more and more of the change to the process, they take pride in its success and in their ownership.
- Generate capacity for continuous improvement. The participants will get more efficient and thorough at documenting, changing, and creating processes as they gain experience.

Effective facilitation of *kaizen* events builds Lean culture in multiple layers. First, the team members learn skills, techniques and principles, which form the basis of a culture of continuous improvement. Secondly, they achieve concrete gains in the value of their daily work, increasing their job satisfaction. Ultimately, these team members join the ranks of those eager to apply the principles in large and small ways throughout the organization. Conversely, a negative experience in a *kaizen* project can spread a negative view of Lean, jeopardizing the initiative's forward momentum. Green Belt training prepares individuals for these responsibilities.

MODULE I—FACILITATION SKILLS

Qualities of a Good Facilitator

- Trust in other people and their capacities
- Patience and good listening skills
- Self-awareness and openness to learning new skills
- Confidence without arrogance
- Respect for the opinions of others
- Practice in creative and innovative thinking
- Flexibility in changing methods and sequences
- Knowledge of group development, including the ability to sense a group's mood and change methods or adjust the program on the spot
- A good sense of the utilization of space and materials for optimal participation

Instruction for participant self-assessment: Which of these skills do you currently possess? Identify areas that you would like to gain in proficiency or strengthen your existing skills. Keep these notes to refer to throughout the program, and revisit at the close of the program.

Team Dynamics and Decision Making

Teams have a common purpose, shared goals, and shared outcomes (risks and rewards). Further, there are specific roles for each member, creating a collaborative interdependency with structure and rules.

Bruce Tuckman's model[1] for the stages of small group development is directly applicable to most Lean project teams. *The Lean Handbook* explains the relationship of this model to the dynamics of facilitating a *kaizen* event: "as the team develops maturity and ability, relationships are established, and the leader changes leadership style. The leader begins with directing; moves through coaching, participating, finishing, and delegating; and ends with almost detached."[2] Below is a brief description of each stage:

- Forming: The polite stage. Members trying to define the task. Lofty, conceptual discussions as people try to express who they are. Discussions about what information needs to be gathered

- Storming: The "bid for power" stage. Members begin to show their true styles. A growing impatience will surface over lack of progress. Members will get into one another's territory, causing irritation. General disagreement over process, task, and overall purpose of the team.
- Norming: The working-together stage. Ground rules and procedures that may have been overlooked are now taken more seriously. Less time will be spent on idea generation, and more on decision-making. Members will want to limit agenda items to focus on specific topics. Subgroups may be formed to move along faster. Conflicts are addressed and resolved.
- Performing: The effective team stage. Be productive! Tasks will be accomplished, and the team will look for more to do. Be proactive, and not necessarily wait for direction from management. Demonstrate loyalty to the group, and respect individual dissension and disagreement.
- Adjourning/reforming: Team goals/objectives have been met. Team introduced to new targets or objectives. Roles in the implementation & follow-up on current project.

It is worth noting that not all teams move through these stages in a linear fashion. For example, a performing team might regress into a storming stage as they struggle with the final details required to complete their task.

Group Dynamics and Personality Types

Any time a group of people works together, there are dynamics such as the history of the group, subgroupings and individual members, group norms, and informal and formal leadership within the group. As a facilitator, you are responsible for navigating those dynamics. People in the same workplace see things differently, and personality traits influence behavior on a Lean team as well as in the workplace.

While diversity of type strengthens teams and organizations, facilitators should understand how different personality preferences could impact team dynamics. Green Belts do not need to categorize the personality type of team members. Rather, you should always assume that your team is comprised of different personality types; respecting their needs will maximize the group's effectiveness. Consider the following:

- The introverts on your team need time to process. Even if the high-energy, fast-paced extroverts want to keep working, their fellow team members need some quiet time. Just because the introverts are not talking doesn't mean they're not paying attention. Make sure you take breaks and enforce ground rules about interrupting and talking over one another.
- The team members whose personality preferences tend toward thinking and judging should not be assumed to be resisters just because they're asking questions and challenging assumptions. They can help to strength the team's work. They will see the value in the use of metrics, which can be persuasive in the sell and in building Lean culture.
- The team members who have personality preferences in intuition see the big picture and the possibilities ahead. They can help the others see the empowering potential of Lean culture.

While it can be challenging to guide a diverse team, the product will better than one generated by a team with "group think." It's useful to keep that in mind as you learn to manage a range of behaviors.

Strategies and Techniques for Facilitators

Facilitation skills require constant adaptation. You want everyone to participate, but you also need to keep the discussion relevant. Some people might need to be asked to speak more briefly or less frequently. Others will need to be encouraged to voice their opinions. Use active listening: make eye contact, stay focused, acknowledge input, stay present—think about what they're saying—not what you're going to say next.

While encouraging the expression of various viewpoints, the more important the decision, the more critical it is to have all pertinent information—facts, not simply opinions.

Ask neutral, open-ended questions to encourage team members to open up and give more information about their work. Open-ended questions start with "Why," "How," "What," or "Tell me about..." For example: "What do you think about this problem?" "What has been your experience on this type of problem?"

To draw people out: "Has anyone else ever had that experience? Tell us more about that; how does it work?"

To encourage more participation: "How does what we have been saying so far sound to the rest of you? What other aspects of the problem have we missed?" "Can anyone suggest what information we need at this stage?"

To limit overactive participation: "You've made several interesting observations. Does anyone else want to add to them?"

Call attention to strong disagreements. When handled openly, differences of opinion yield creative solutions.

Ask people to speak for themselves and to be specific. Do not allow statements like, "Some people seem to feel…" or "What he/she is trying to say is…" Encourage people to use "I" statements.

Ask focused closed-ended questions to elicit specific information. They start with "Who," "When," "How much," and so forth.

Repeat back to clarify. Example: "You said that it takes a long time … how long does it typically take?"

Summarize to move the group forward and refocus dialogue. To keep the discussion moving: "Do you think we have spent enough time on this phase of the problem? Can we move on to another part of it?" An optional code word to utilize is ELMO (Enough, Let's Move On).

Facilitating Problem Situations

A team member abdicates: not offering ideas or comments, responding tersely to questions, accompanied by body language such as folded arms, or sitting apart from the group. Potential strategies: Give the person responsibility for a task; ask the person an open-ended question ("John, what do you think about this?"), talk with the person offline; describe the behavior you have observed, and ask open-ended questions to determine what is going on. It's possible that it has nothing to do with the project.

A team member dominates: speaking up at every opportunity, speaking forcefully to persuade others or exert control, not listening to others' ideas, taking the lead on every group activity without waiting to be asked; making eye contact only with those who support him/her as leader. Potential strategies: Consistently refer to the rules whenever someone's behavior deviates from the rules, ask direct questions to the quieter members to balance the conversation, courteously interrupt the dominant person and allow someone else to speak. Act as traffic controller, remind all members of their roles and responsibilities, and talk with the offender offline; describe the behavior you have observed and its impact.

Teams get into conflict: If there are unproductive debates over how to get something done, tension between individuals, sarcasm, eye-rolling, personal attacks and put-downs, expressions of frustration and impatience, not listening to each other, inability to reach consensus and implement a strategy. Potential strategies: Encourage members to focus on each other's point of view by asking questions and repeating back. Ask each to point out the positive aspects of the other's position. Engage the group in brainstorming solutions that meet specific criteria. Ex: "In the next 3 minutes, generate ten ideas for ways we can avoid bottlenecking all travel requests in the finance department." Use structured decision-making techniques described in the next section to select an option. Talk to each of the disagreeing parties individually; describe the behavior you observed; ask each to commit to professionally appropriate collaborative behavior.

Guiding the Team to Consensus

Facilitators guide teams to complete their tasks without quashing discussion. Confirm understanding and agreements. Example: "Am I right in thinking that we have reached agreement on this point? We seem to be moving toward a decision now, so can we consider what it will mean if we decide it this way?" Examples of group decision-making techniques are listed below:

- Brainstorming—to generate ideas capturing the entire team's input and creativity. Instructions: Clarify topic to be brainstormed. Ideas are called out randomly "popcorn-style" without critique or discussion—the goal is quantity, not quality. Capture key words and phrases on a flip chart or white board.
- Nominal Group Technique (Round Robin)—to ensure all team members have equal opportunity to express ideas, viewpoints and interests. Instructions: Clarify the topic, set a time limit, and each person silently writes down ideas. Call on each team member in turn, taking one idea from each. Record the input on a flip chart or ask individuals to post their ideas using sticky notes. Continue collecting ideas, while allowing people to "pass" if all their ideas have been used.
- Affinity Diagram—Team members write ideas on sticky notes and place them on a wall. Team members (or 1–2 people) sort the items in a way that makes sense logically and conceptually. Label categories

with a header for each category. Note: This technique can be very helpful in organizing the bright ideas during a *kaizen* event.

- N/3—Organizes list of ideas by focusing on the "critical few"—where the team has the most interest and energy. Instructions: Generate lots of ideas. Divide total number of ideas (N) by 3, which determines number of choices for each person. Team members write down their choices. They cast their votes for their choices by using colored dots or sticky notes.

- Advocate—The opportunity for individual team members to publicly recommend an idea allows the team to consider other points of view in selecting best options. People share their thinking, without anyone interrupting with "Yeah, but…" Tip: Ask participants to address their remarks to the facilitator rather than to each other, or it can deteriorate into a debate. Example: "I'd like to give everyone a chance to do a brief commercial (1–2 min) for any idea that you want to see on the final list or anything that you don't."

- Straw Poll—A quick check-in to determine the team's views on a particular issue. Ask for a quick show of hands to demonstrate willingness to accept an idea, item or solution. Example: "We've talked a lot about item 'X.' I'd just like to do a straw poll to find out where people are about this idea. By a show of hands, how many would be willing to have 'X' be one of our final choices? How many simply could not live with this on the list?"

- Consensus Building—The agreement of all team members to support the decision is confirmed when all team members can state the following after a decision is made: "I believe you understand my point of view." "I believe I understand your point of view." "Even though this may not be the way I would decide things all by myself, I will support the decision 100% because it was arrived at in an open and fair manner." "I will support the team's decision outside the meeting."

MODULE II—FACILITATING A *KAIZEN* EVENT

Facilitation of *kaizen* events requires attention to both process and product. A good facilitator guides the team in accomplishing each task, while taking the time to assure that each member's perspectives are heard. There is a skill to eliciting participation without allowing the team to get stuck arguing or telling irrelevant stories.

While developing your own style in the balance between product and process, consider the following:

- Excessive focus on product shortchanges the process. Lean practitioners can get caught up on "the lure of content." Given your experience and commitment to Lean, you may identify an optimal future state and be tempted to drive the team on that path. You risk losing the team's confidence if you advocate for a solution. If they go along to adopt your solution, they have not gained the skills and confidence they need for future Lean projects.
- Excessive focus on process shortchanges the product. The future state must be a team product, so facilitators should remain purposefully neutral. However, the Lean event may fail if the team chooses too safe a path. Certain workplace cultures result in risk adverse team composition, particularly if the team lacks a participant in the role of "fresh eyes." If the future state is too similar to the current state, the team members may think their time was wasted, and the sponsor will be unlikely to charter new projects. The word gets around and it could inhibit the growth of Lean culture.

The right mix: you have a responsibility to challenge the status quo *and* teach the team how to design a Lean future state. You'll also be teaching them about Lean.

Facilitator as Lean instructor: Green Belts learn to work with teams that are new to Lean by providing instruction on both techniques and principles. As you meet your team, you can assure them that Lean is easy to use and virtually intuitive. Even if you're facilitating a Lean team during a Yellow Belt class where the primary instructor presents the core material, you'll still be helping your team understand and apply Lean principles and techniques.

Facilitator's Responsibilities Pre-event

- Charter development with the sponsor: Identify the process, the scope, team composition, and a draft problem statement. Define success and deliverables.

- Bring materials including mapping paper, painter's tape, scotch tape, sticky notes, markers, and flip chart paper.
- Determine the map location and team location—sitting in a V shape or U shape facing the map? Where will you be—will you work the board or select team member(s) to do so as you facilitate the group from other vantage points? Will you alternate as needed?

Facilitator's Responsibilities Post-event

- Generally, the facilitator's primary job ends when the implementation plan is presented to the sponsor. Once the sponsor approves the plan, the sponsor and the team leader/project manager are responsible to assure that the project is implemented. Either the facilitator, the data manager or the team leader should prepare the A3 report for the team and the agency's Lean coordinator.
- Optional: create an electronic version of the maps using E-Draw freeware, Visio, or other software (Some agencies assign this function to a data manager; others do not use e-versions.).
- The facilitator and the agency's Lean coordinator should be copied on updates from the team's 30/60/90-day check-ins. If the project falters, the Lean coordinator may need to work with the project manager and the sponsor to get it back on track. As the project is implemented, Lean coordinator and the team track the metrics and communicate the gains to build Lean culture.

Overview and Summary

- Before the Lean event: the facilitator and sponsor meet to draft the charter and select the team.
- Starting the event: establish ground rules, roles, expectations, data management.
- During the event: guide the team to complete the task; consulting with the sponsor, as appropriate. Schedule the sell.
- Closing the event: confirm responsibility of the project manager and team members for the implementation plan. Schedule the 30/60/90-day reviews, with a communication commitment by all team members, including fresh eyes.

Sample Lean Project Schedule

GBs may be asked to facilitate as part of the Yellow Belt training program, or in *kaizen* events on-site in agencies. On-site projects are generally half-day sessions (3–4 half-days, all in the same week). Yellow Belt sessions generally run 3 full days over a 2-week period, or on 3 consecutive days.

Pre-Training	Day 1	Day 2	Day 3	Post-Training
Identify sponsor, facilitator(s) Select team Draft charter Facilitator meets with team leader/ project manager	Introduction to Lean Chartering *kaizen* Set up the swim lanes, and start mapping the current state Wrap-up Optional calibration meeting: the facilitator & project manager meet with the sponsor	Introduce the data sheets Complete the current state map, with data sheets, bright ideas & assumptions Introduce the A3 template and the summary sheet Map the future state Data manager: begin work on the A3 report. Optional: prepare an e-version of the maps	Introduce the impact-effort grid and the implementation plan Complete the future state, the impact-effort grid, the implementation plan, and the communication plan Plan the sell. Data manager: complete the A3 report, and update the charter. Optional: prepare an e-version of the maps.	Team "sell" to the sponsor (can also be held on Day 3 of YB training) Expect a two-week response time for the sponsor to approval plan implementation Decisions on timeline for action, deliverables & 30/60/90-day reviews Measure results, communicate and celebrate
Sponsor Driven	Facilitated	Facilitated	Facilitated	Project manager-driven

The following is a checklist that summarizes the primary activities of a facilitator during a *kaizen* event. Appendix C contains a more detailed set of instructions that is used for GBs who are facilitating project teams during a Yellow Belt class.

LEAN FACILITATOR CHECKLIST

Prior to the Session
- Meet with the sponsor to review the charter, team composition, the goal(s), and timeline.
- Have materials and an adequate space for the process mapping.

Starting Session
- Introduce yourself, the basic principles of Lean and the role of the team and the sponsor.
- Develop Ground Rules and post on flip chart paper.
- Review the charter and explain the timeline for the project and the tasks ahead (e.g. map the current state and design a future state). Post the problem statement and the end-user customer on flip chart paper.
- Explain the color or shape codes for the sticky notes, and the concept of "bright ideas."
- Post the swim lanes on the left side of the map.
- Ask a team member to write the name of each step on a yellow sticky note.
- Place the steps in sequence, according to the team's understanding of the current state. *Alternative approach*: ask a team member to do this task.

Ending a Session
- Summarize the progress, praise the work, and provide critical feedback.
- Assign research homework and ask the team to invite subject matter experts, if appropriate.

Beginning each Subsequent Session
- Open by asking team members to share their thoughts and feedback since the last meeting.
- Review the work plan for the day and describe what lies ahead to complete the project.

Metrics and Value-added Assessment of the Current State
- Introduce the data sheets and the importance of measuring work time and cycle time.

- Identify a team member to write on the data sheets.
- Ask the team to evaluate the value of each step using color codes. Remind the team that this is not a value judgment about the employees doing the work.
- Ask a team member to prepare the summary table on flip chart paper.

Preparing for the Future State, the Implementation Plan and the Sell

- Review each "bright idea" as you guide the team to complete the future state.
- Ask a team member to write data sheets and summarize metrics for the future state.
- Identify all tasks required to implement the future state in the quadrants of easy to do/big improvement; easy to do/small improvement; hard to do/big improvement; hard to do/small improvement.
- Complete the implementation plan grid. Ask the team if they want to recommend a phased approach—be specific about all tasks and timelines.
- Confirm the project manager/team leader is responsible for follow-up.
- Work with the team to prepare an A3 report of the project.
- Plan the "sell" to the sponsor, with a role for each team member.

Post Event

- Finalize the A3 report and send it to your organization's Lean coordinator.
- Check back with the team at the 30-day mark to confirm the implementation is on schedule. Contact the Lean coordinator to assist the project manager/team leader and sponsor, if necessary.

MODULE III—CHANGE MANAGEMENT AND LEAN MANAGEMENT

While much of the program prepares Green Belts (GBs) to facilitate *kaizen* events, the topics of change management and overall Lean management are essential components. The use of tools must be linked to the application in management. In *Toyota Kata*, Mike Rother said, "We should be clear: Projects and workshops ≠ continuous improvement."[3] Rother explains that "Toyota's visible tools and techniques are built upon invisible management thinking and routines."[4]

While developing an understanding of the multifaceted nature of Lean, GBs consider the dynamics that impede traditional managers from embracing change. Managers seldom work directly on products—they do not necessarily add value, according to the Lean definition (activities valued by the customer). In a traditional management role, mid-level managers are dealing with crises. In this reactive mode, it is difficult to get in front of each new crisis. They suffer from the *muri* of management.

GBs can help them move from traditional management to Lean management, but it is not an easy path. Processes must be stabilized before they can be improved. As processes are stabilized and variation is reduced, errors will decrease, and there will be fewer crises. As standard work is developed, there is a baseline from which to improve. Then, the manager's role is to support the employees who are making the improvements.

GBs can help middle managers to transform their role, assisting them to charter *kaizen* events, conduct *gemba* walks, organize 5S opportunities, sponsor and conduct Lean projects. GBs can guide mid-level managers to understand their critical role in enabling employees to engage in continuous improvement, to get the best customer value using the fewest resources.

Exercise: How do you define process excellence? Identify the primary processes used in your unit or organization. Rate the processes

- According to your definition of excellence
- From management's perspective
- From rank and file employees' perspective
- From the customers' perspective

Consider the role of the boss. While Lean relies upon front line workers to optimize customer value, and mid-level managers to charter *kaizen* events, the boss also has a critical role. It's quite different from the role that traditional managers play. GBs need to understand Lean management, and the role for both middle management and top management. This dynamic will be discussed in detail in Chapter 7.

Managing Change

Since Lean practitioners are natural change agents, it's common to become frustrated and judgmental about those who you perceive as resistant to change. GBs should understand that there are several reasons for resistance that can be remedied with best practices at various stages. Good communication is fundamental to addressing concerns. It's also critical to have clarity, transparency, and inclusiveness in the planning.

Despite a clear message, people may resist if the appeal is based on narrow personal reasons, and/or there is a lack of respect and trust in the change initiator. Resistance may occur if the habit patterns of the work group are ignored, the cost is too high, or the reward for making the change is seen as inadequate, and the present situation seems satisfactory. Paradoxically, the fear of failure or fear of success may each be factors. There may be concerns about increased work demands or the pressure of learning new skills that may be required for the redesigned process.

The team-based structure allows GBs to guide the participants to a consensus solution. Generally, though, not everyone in the workplace serves on the team. Often, there are those impacted by the proposed future state who did not experience the collective decision making. They are looking at it through a personal lens—how does the change affect me? Even the event sponsors may lose their nerve to support change if employees are vocal in their opposition. The team's communication plan must anticipate and address these concerns.

Project selection, team composition, sponsor commitment, and consistent communication are critical. GBs can look to work by John Kotter, Kurt Lewin, and Torben Rick to go more deeply into the topic of change management.[5] Below is a summary of strategies.

- Communicate the vision and the plan
- Involve and empower affected parties
- Create short-term wins—build confidence and credibility
- Take on a manageable number of initiatives
- Don't let up—foster and encourage determination and persistence—ongoing change—ongoing progress reporting—highlight achievements
- Sustain the changes
- Reinforce the value of change by recruiting and promoting change leaders

- Weave change into culture and build a culture of continuous improvement

Exercise: Work at your tables to answer the following questions. Refer to the Lean initiative in one or more of your organizations.

Team #1—Why is change necessary? What are the most compelling reasons for the change? Can you make a business case for the change? What's the best way to establish a sense of urgency?

Team #2—Identify the barriers to successful implementation of change and propose a countermeasure for each.

Team #3—Who will feel threatened by the change, and how will we deal with their concerns?

Team #4—How well do people trust their leadership? Who are the informal leaders who can help advocate for the change?

TOPICS FOR IN-CLASS DISCUSSION OR HOMEWORK

Options for instructor: Set up the room with separate tables for groups of 4–5 participants each. Assign different topics to each table. Allow 10 minutes for discussion and 5 minutes to summarize into bullet points on flip chart paper. Share in report-out sessions at different points during the training, OR assign as homework, so participants prepare their responses for a quick debriefing session.

Topic #1: How do you select a team for a *kaizen* event? How does the team culture affect the *kaizen* event? How does a facilitator understand and use the team culture to enhance a Lean event?

Topic #2: How do you identify a Lean facilitator for a *kaizen* event? Should you facilitate in your own agency? Do you have a "dog in the fight?" Is the sponsor in your chain of command? How can you access the network of Green Belts to find an outside facilitator?

Topic #3: How do you evaluate the performance of a Lean event? How do Lean events fail? How do Lean events succeed?

Topic #4: How do you cultivate employee ownership of process improvement? How do you create a clear and compelling case for change?

How do you keep your Lean peers motivated? How do you keep yourself motivated?

Topic #5: How do you develop a consistent approach and tools for implementing Lean? How do you sustain your Lean skills and knowledge? How do you build the infrastructure for change?

Topic for all: How do you choose where to focus your improvement efforts? How do you set clear goals? How do you provide visible support for process improvement efforts? How do you link Lean improvement events to agency mission and strategy?

MODULE IV—LEAN TOOLS, SKILLS, AND RESOURCES

The practice of Lean is more than making process maps. Lean practitioners seek to build a culture of continuous improvement. If a third of the staff are change agents, a third are on the fence, and a third are resisters, the change agents can prevail if they can influence those on the fence in a positive direction. Remember to cultivate courage and foster appropriate risk-taking.

Typically, analyzing a process calls for a 3- to 5-day *kaizen* event. However, there are situations where, as a GB, you may choose another Lean tool, and you should be familiar with a range of Lean tools. Revisit the term *kaizen* in its generic meaning. As Jim Womack noted, the purpose of *kaizen* is to "create stability and sustainability in the bottom of the organization where value is actually created."[6]

Using its broad definition, there are many types of *kaizen* activities. The 5S provides a structured format for organizing a work area. Like the process mapping event, it seeks to make measured and documented improvement.

Consider "just do it" *kaizens* when the participants brainstorm fast changes and adjustments. There is no standard time frame for these events, but it is important to document the changes and their effect, and any savings in time or other resources.

The EPA's *Lean Government Methods Guide*[7] provides an overview of tools and suggests when each might be suitable for various goals and circumstances. For simple, structured methods, the guide suggests "daily Lean" methods such as 5S, standard work, and visual controls. Mini-Leans can include process walks that identify immediate fixes. Structured team events range from a half-day to 5 days, commonly using process mapping.

The guide notes that successful projects require substantial prep and follow-up. The same is true for the more complex challenge of process design, to establish standard work where no formal process previously existed. Among the advanced Lean methods is strategy deployment, which seeks to align improvement initiatives to the organization's strategic goals.

All tools are based on the fundamental problem-solving methodology of PDCA: Plan–Do–Check–Act/Adjust. Or, PDSA: Plan–Do–Study—Act/Adjust.

GBs should spend time in the *gemba*, to observe and talk with those touching the problem. Look for root causes. Practice patience. While change agents are naturally eager to suggest solutions, it is not your place to decide for others. The *gemba* walk is not a visit by an efficiency expert. It is an opportunity to see and understand. As the work team identifies root causes and develops countermeasures, the PDCA cycle reminds us that no problem is solved forever; countermeasures can create new problems.

Lean tools for metrics and root cause analysis are discussed in Chapter 6.

Terminology

Since Lean developed organically across many public and private sector enterprises, there is variation in terminology and technique among practitioners. Charter templates and data collection tools vary. As practitioners work across silos, there will be some *muda* as they adjust to the differences.

For example, the terms "process mapping" and "value stream mapping" are sometimes used interchangeably. In Lean manufacturing, however, processes are subsets of value streams. According to *The Lean Handbook*, a value stream is "a set of actions required to take a specific product from raw material to finished good."[8] *Kaizen* events generally use process mapping to improve sections of value streams.

As GBs from different training programs gain experience and read more about Lean, they will notice differences in the nomenclature, but the core concepts and underlying principles remain the same.

Video and YouTube Clips

TED Talks: Simon Sinek's "How Great Leaders Inspire Action"[9] and Derek Sivers' "How to Start a Movement"[10] can be viewed in class or as a homework assignment. Sinek describes the diffusion of innovation and Sivers demonstrates the critical role of early adopters.

DVD—Womack on Lean Management.[11] The entire seminar is too long to show in class, but you can select some highlights to emphasize the key points. It's available for purchase from the Lean Enterprise Institute. LEI webinars and free YouTube postings are also available on a range of topics. www.lean.org.

Process Mapping Software

While some Lean practitioners keep their maps for reference until the future state is completed, many prefer to create electronic versions. On the other hand, posting the current and future state maps in the workplace could be a visual management tool to ensure accountability. Leave the map up until the project is implemented.

Archive an e-version of the process maps. Once implemented, the "future state" becomes the new current state—documented standard workflow. Some practitioners use Visio or other software. Black Belt Heather Barto uses the free ware version of E-Draw Mind Map[12] and she conducts workshops for NH Lean practitioners to learn to use the tool.

COMPLETING THE GREEN BELT PROGRAM

Exercise

- Assess your organization's Lean capacity and consider how the projects you will facilitate can fit into the larger Lean initiative. Does your organization have a Lean coordinator and other trained Lean facilitators? If so, how will you join in? If not, what's your plan? Is there a method to seek input and select Lean projects? If not, what's your plan?
- Review your self-assessment from Day 1. Summarize the learning from the class that related to your initial goals. Identify the gaps. Renew those goals and establish new goals. Are you ready to facilitate?

Plan for your practicum: Facilitate or co-facilitate a *kaizen* event and submit an A3 report to your agency's Lean coordinator and to BET faculty. Options include facilitating a project team at an upcoming Yellow Belt class or at an event in your organization.

SUMMARY OF LESSONS LEARNED

- The Green Belt program is structured similarly to the Yellow Belt program, with the integration of theory and practice.
- GB skills are developed by practice. It's critical to provide ongoing training for a growing cadre of Lean practitioners who are committed change agents. The program must include mentoring, feedback, and accountability mechanisms to support the development of rookie GBs. Becoming a Lean practitioner is not a "set it and forget it." Completion of a 3-day class is just the start.
- GBs should not facilitate projects in their own work units. As Sam said, they shouldn't "have a dog in the fight." Develop reciprocal facilitator swaps among agencies and work units within agencies. GBs need management support for this flexibility.
- Black Belt Heather Barto summarized, "Key ingredients for a successful Lean event include: invested leadership that supports the plan to improve as well as innovate, and dedicated staff that are encouraged to think freely to come up with outside of the box ideas. An open mind is pivotal. Change can be a challenge, but if it's done with people and not for them, the uptake can be quite successful."

APPLYING THE LESSONS

- Build a robust Green Belt program with a combination of hands-on practice of facilitation techniques and a range of Lean tools.
- Include a component on Lean management, so GBs learn that it's not about the maps.
- Provide continuing education workshops with opportunities to practice using the tools.
- Assist rookie GBs in identifying an experienced practitioner who will serve as a mentor, and a facilitation opportunity that will allow them to try out their skills. Following the practice facilitation, the rookies should debrief with their mentors, reviewing the A3 report from the event, and discussing lessons learned.
- Schedule rookie GBs as facilitators during Yellow Belt programs to provide a structured opportunity to build their skills and confidence.

- Encourage facilitator swaps among agencies so that GBs gain experience and avoid facilitating in their own units.
- Create networking opportunities, as part of the continuing education workshops or as stand-alone events. As GBs gain more experience, they will learn from one another, preparing to mentor future GBs.

NOTES

1 Bruce W. Tuckman, "Developmental Sequence in Small Groups," *Psychological Bulletin*, 1965, **63** (6): 384–399.
2 Anthony Manos and Chad Vincent, Editors, *The Lean Handbook* (ASQ Quality Press, Milwaukee, WI, 2012) 39.
3 Mike Rother, *Toyota Kata* (McGraw-Hill Education, 2010) 11.
4 Mike Rother, *Toyota Kata* (McGraw-Hill Education, 2010) 5.
5 References for this section include John Kotter's Leading Change, Kurt Lewin's Torben Rick. Accessed April 22, 2018. www.TorbenRick.EU.
6 Jim Womack, *Gemba Walks* (The Lean Enterprise Institute, Cambridge, 2011) 101.
7 "Lean in Government Methods Guide," United States Environmental Protection Agency. Accessed April 7, 2017. www2.epa.gov/lean/lean-government-methods-guide.
8 Anthony Manos and Chad Vincent (Eds.), *The Lean Handbook* (ASQ Quality Press, Milwaukee, WI, 2012) 393.
9 Simon Sinek, "How Great Leaders Inspire Action" (TED: Ideas Worth Spreading, September 2009). Accessed April 20, 2018. www.ted.com/talks/lang/en/simon_sinek_how_great_leaders_inspire_action.html.
10 Derek Sivers, "How to Start a Movement" (TED: Ideas Worth Spreading, February 2010). Accessed April 20, 2018. www.ted.com/talks/derek_sivers_how_to_start_a_movement.html.
11 Womack on Lean Management. James P. Womack. DVD. (Lean Enterprise Institute, Inc., January 11, 2010). www.lean.org/BookStore/ProductDetails.cfm?SelectedProductId=263.
12 Edraw Mind Map. Accessed April 21, 2018. www.edrawsoft.com/MindMap.php.

5

How to Get Away with Muda

How can we learn from our failures? This chapter examines cases where the *muda* won. Losses in these cases compounded the *muri* of the employees. There are many drivers of intractable *muda*; this chapter looks at a series of those common to the public sector.

Muda can be found embedded in processes that are essential to service and regulatory functions. Those processes can be improved. In other instances, an entire process is *muda*. Archaic processes remain in place because no one has stopped them. When considering the intransigence of the latter, a quote from Peter Drucker comes to mind: "There is surely nothing quite so useless as doing great efficiently what should not be done at all."[1] Thus, Lean should not be used to find ways to do dumb things faster, but it can be used to identify the purpose of each process and the value of each step within.

Muda #1: A legacy process. "The way it's always been done." Even when it's widely known that the process is a problem, a combination of *muri* (when overburdened staff don't have the time or permission to stop to re-design the process), risk aversion, and organizational inertia makes it easier to keep the process in place than to replace it.

Multi-layered approval processes typically fall into this category. The out-of-state travel approval process is a common example. Administrators have the illusory comfort of control, presuming that requiring a series of sign-offs protects the organization. Reinforced by fear of a bad outcome, such processes are very difficult to dislodge. Even managers who espouse Lean are susceptible to a nagging trepidation that if the process as we know it goes away, there might be a negative consequence for which blame will be assigned. The out-of-state travel approval process is discussed again in Chapter 6, and a hypothetical project based on this scenario is in Appendix B.

Muda #2: **A process created in response to a single negative event**. An administrator adds one or more layers of control, "so that (fill in the blank) will never happen again"

Risk-averse, politically sensitive administrators tend to add new layers of checking whenever something goes wrong. Managers see a problem and try to think of a way to prevent it from ever happening again. Legislators have the same tendency.

A scenario is used in the Green Belt class is based on such a situation, so trainees can practice dealing with change management challenges that are common to Lean efforts in bureaucracies. The exercise is based on a process that should have been discontinued. It remained in place because a manager could point to a single negative incident as justification for the process. The incident was the result of individual misconduct. Rather than deal with the individual, redundant checking was established. Staff in the work unit developed a comfort level for the process for various reasons. An administrator, reluctant to make a unilateral decision to discontinue the process, agreed to sponsor a Lean event. The event failed to end the process. Rather than identifying the process as lacking in value, the team reached a compromise leading to modest improvements in efficiency.

During the exercise based on this scenario, Green Belt trainees practice dealing with a range of personalities who have different concerns and priorities. It is instructive to see how the exercise plays out, and the lessons learned when the trainees debrief. We close the session by applying Drucker's observation to conclude that making *muda* go faster is still *muda*.

There is a sample charter for the event, details on roles and the exercise instructions in Appendix D.

Muda #3, with *Muri*: The combination of a diffusion of responsibility and the failure to align structural accountability with adequate staffing levels is sadly persistent.

Sometimes, the organization is just missing one staff position: the person responsible for coordinating a key function. Unlike the private sector, which can add positions based on business need, public-sector budgeting processes make it difficult to add a new position when an unanticipated opportunity arises mid-cycle.

Staff does their best to collaborate to fill the gaps, but peer groups lack the authority to conduct business. Employees try to work collaboratively in a seemingly endless series of coordination meetings. Monuments of *muda* and *muri*.

Our Lean failure in this category was a project to roll out online learning. In 2014, a project team in the Certified Public Manager program studied the use of a learning management system (LMS) as an online supplement to traditional classroom training. They found that a hybrid model, mixing interactive classroom skill practices with online resources, would be a cost-effective way to expand the availability of training. The team recommended the use of Moodle, a free LMS. Two Lean projects were conducted.

One project examined training. A multi-agency team documented the current state of training, finding lots of non-standard rework, time, and travel expense. For example, all agencies were required to provide training on the state's sexual harassment prevention policy. Many created their own programs (rework), while others simply required employees to sign the policy attesting that they had read it. Some agencies paid out-stationed staff to travel to a central office for a briefing on the policy. The Lean team contrasted these costs with the use of one standard on-line program.

The second project examined the alignment of IT resources between the statewide IT agency and the individual agencies for the use of shared Moodle classrooms. The future state map indicated that an enterprise solution could be established in 6 months for internal users (state employees). The external server would be available 6 months later. The cost was estimated at $1,100 to start, with $800/year required to maintain the system.

A multi-agency group of committed individuals met regularly. Work began, but soon stalled because the staff remained decentralized, each responsible for other priorities. Unanticipated obstacles arose, and no one person was responsible for managing the project.

Ironically, we were nominated for an Extraordinary Service Award, which is intended "to recognize state employees who perform a service in their jobs that goes above and beyond the call of duty or who make suggestions that raise revenue or save costs." Governor Hassan and the Executive Council recognized ten employees from five different agencies for their work to develop online training.

> November 18, 2015: Recognition to the members of the Moodle Oversight Team for their vision and commitment in the development of a statewide learning management system.
>
> The Team represents a statewide collaboration of state employees with training- and technology-related positions. Their initiative evolved into a cost-effective, centralized, and sustainable model that will transform

training and education for State of New Hampshire employees and external customers based on best practices of training and education. This system will reduce travel and training costs and will provide access to consistent online training.

Unfortunately, although the Moodle technology was free and available, only three of the agencies were able to use it. Lacking a statewide coordinator, each agency was on its own. Those with resources created their own programs on their own servers. Only one agency, DOS, had the resources to maximize the value of online training.

We didn't give up easily, though. In a goodwill workaround, one of the award recipients, Rob Kelley (DAS), partnered with Jessie Webb (DOS), who had created a training program on the Sexual Harassment Policy. Rob was an IT specialist with access to the platform, and he was able to post Jessie's program on Moodle.

However, there was more *muda* at Moodle. Lacking a statewide Moodle coordinator, or staff for a Moodle Helpdesk, few knew how to access the platform. The Department of Information Technology (DOIT) did not have a position available to support the initiative. BET's part-time instructional designer lacked the authority to coordinate resources or the capacity to provide the IT support. The extraordinary service was once again thwarted by *muda* and our spirits nearly crushed by *muri*.

Basic *muda*: BET, the statewide training unit, has only one full-time professor for a workforce of 10,000. Repeated requests for appropriate staffing are denied. Agencies hire their own training staff, if they have the resources to do so, often creating redundant programs. Also, some agencies send their staff to expensive and time-consuming out-of-state trainings, which could be offered by the state's training unit if resources were adequate. Agencies without resources go without training. This *muda* resulted in substantial *muri*, leading to staff turnover, and further *muda*.

In *Gemba Kaizen*, Masaaki Imai defines *muri* as "human strain on the job." For example, "workers not equipped with enough skills to perform their jobs will feel strained."[2] *The Lean Handbook* acknowledges that while *muri* is generally mentioned after *muda* and *mura*, "it is perhaps the most critical to reduce because overburden (*muri*) can lead to or cause waste (*muda*) or fluctuation (*mura*) ... It means pushing people and systems beyond their normal limits."[3]

Imai explains the significance of training in the reduction *muri* (which, in turn, reduces *muda* and *mura*): "When workers do not understand the value they are providing to their customers, they will create more waste and cost. To eliminate *muri*, workers as well as managers should be trained to perform their jobs."[4]

Extreme *muda*: The training staff from different agencies continued to meet to try to figure out how to launch the Moodle initiative. Regardless of the number of times we met, the obstacle remained the same. None of us had the power, authority, or capacity to act outside of our own agencies. The amount of work hours spent in meetings to try to figure it out was, as one award recipient described, "pushing dirt around"—a vicious cycle of *muda, muri,* and *mura.*

We tried not to let it defeat us. Although the goal of using the platform for a comprehensive range of topics remained stalled in 2017, agencies were using the online Sexual Harassment Policy and Cybersecurity Policy Training. I kept my copy of the award posted over my desk as a reminder of this failed project. It spurred me on to work with DES Lean coordinator Dan Hrobak to prepare an introductory Lean White Belt program. Since neither Dan nor I are instructional designers, this initial program was just a couple of modules of rudimentary voiceover PowerPoints with some attachments. It was posted on Moodle in the fall of 2017, 2 years after we received the Extraordinary Service Award.[5] The agenda for Lean White Belt is in Appendix A.

Trying not to let the *muda* keep us down, the Lean Executive Committee had been promoting the White Belt training, with sporadic growth in the number of participants for the first 6 months it was available. Then, there was a breakthrough of creative initiative. During his Black Belt program, Sgt. Tom Lencki of the State Police conducted a Lean education and awareness project during which 82% of sworn and civilian staff took the White Belt online. This example of Lean activism and initiative is a potentially replicable model for other agencies (Figure 5.1).

Muda #4: **Limited Technological Know-How.** Technological limitations are substantial, and passionate commitment is no substitute for expertise. To put it simply: we don't know what we don't know.

At times the gaps are more evident than others. One of our Lean Network members showed me a short video she had made featuring lessons from a recent project. I was very impressed. She commented that her daughter had helped her with it. I responded that I didn't have teenagers at home anymore. My colleague responded, "She's ten."

The incident was an amusing way of realizing that our Lean activists could benefit from training on the basic use of software products.

FIGURE 5.1
Lean Black Belt Sgt. Tom Lencki speaking to the NH Lean Network.

Sometimes we get help from our kids. The daughter of a LEC member designed our logo. But these workarounds include the *muda* of trial and error and the *mura* of uneven quality. It might not be too difficult to produce training videos, on-line seminars, e-versions of our maps, posters of our A3 reports, charts for visual management—perhaps by using software we already own. Most of us are self-taught, working slowly by trial and error, just skimming the surface of what could be achieved. *Muda.* We don't know what we don't know, and we struggle to figure it out. *Muri.*

The lack of technical expertise in communication modes has a minor impact, compared with the impact on major IT projects to operate our enterprises. Frequently, specifications for new IT systems are prepared without considering how the work is done, or why it is done. In the worst-case scenario, a vendor is required to customize the new system to replicate an existing antiquated process. Such approaches are extraordinarily costly and time consuming—calculating the cost of this *muda* in dollars and human effort would be overwhelming. The best way to get ahead of these problems is by using Lean to redesign the workflow first.

The first rule of any technology used in a business process is that automation applied to an efficient process will magnify the efficiency. The second is that automation applied to an inefficient operation will magnify the inefficiency."[6]

Bill Gates

In "Innovate Before You Automate," LeanOhio explains the seven reasons to put process improvement (PI) before IT. The reasons are basic common sense: faster implementation, less customization, easier to maintain, less costly, money spent more wisely, gather preliminary requirements, and create-buy-in. Reason six is the most complicated, and most commonly disregarded:

> Preliminary requirements gathering. As team members are developing a new and improved business process, it's an excellent opportunity to have IT representation in the room. Not only will those IT folks get to hear first-hand dialogue on how the team member night want a new automation system to work for them...but IT staff can share knowledge and set appropriate expectations about infrastructure and platform capabilities.[7]

Public sector organizations often fail to include an IT representative on Lean project teams. Due to chronic short-staffing, IT personnel are generally too busy firefighting to allocate time to *kaizen* events.

IT workers are subject to both components of *muri* (strain and overburden) because of the structure of their work. Masaaki Imai wrote about these challenges in *Gemba Kaizen*. Using a case study, he observed a typical productivity level of 25% due to a series of systemic conditions leaving project managers to compete for resources that were "frequently usurped by others with more influence." Reallocated time was just one source of interruptions driving low productivity. As Imai explained, "For creative workers such as software designers, it is widely accepted that for every interruption—say, a phone call—costs 15 minutes of productivity ... workers were being interrupted four times or more per hour, and consequently had productivity of zero during those periods. In addition, the chaotic schedule resulting from the lack of coordination between teams was causing significant wastes such as work-in-process, rework, and wait time."[8]

With IT staff organized in separate silos; typical sponsors of Lean events lack the authority to assign IT members to project teams. It takes a sponsor with a significant span of control to charter a project with both IT and program staff. When a high-level sponsor authorizes such a *kaizen* event, implementation may falter as the employees return to their silos. The project on Moodle fell apart during the implementation phase because no one with cross-silo authority was tasked with the responsibility to complete the work.

Organizations that automatically include IT representation on Lean projects can avoid unnecessary *muda*. For many, the *muri* of firefighting prevents them from adopting it as a best practice. We'll explore potential paths through the *muri* in Chapter 10.

SUMMARY OF LESSONS LEARNED

- There are many types of *muda* and many causes. While we're working with teams to lean and mistake-proof their processes, new layers of *muda* appear around us. This circumstance creates lots of *muri* for Lean practitioners—it's like someone is drilling holes in our boat. If we can't stop them, we need to learn to bail more quickly. Then *muri* might overtake us, sinking our Lean initiative.
- Revisit the lesson of Chapter 3: it's not about the maps; it's about the management. Were we wrong to expect anything but *muda* and *muri* when we tried to take on big problems without management support and buy-in? Part of me still thinks it was worth the try, but we needed to understand the odds were against us
- "Proceed until apprehended" doesn't always work. As one bureau chief observed, "It's power vs. process." He noted, "You can try to fix the process, but if you don't address the power, you can't fix the process."

APPLYING THE LESSONS

- The *muda* described in this chapter cannot be removed without Lean management. For leaders who have learned traditional management— either in school or on the job—Lean management concepts are counterintuitive. If they're open to learning about it, Chapter 7 contains a "Lean for Leaders" workshop.
- Stay away from ambitious multi-agency projects without solid sponsorship.

- Persistence. Lean activists can fight the *muda* while we're seeking converts at the leadership level. Our colleagues in the Lean movement can help us deal with the *muri*. It boosts our spirits when someone like Sgt. Lencki brings in fresh energy and new ideas. More about that in Chapter 10.

NOTES

1 Peter F. Drucker, "Managing for Business Effectiveness," *Harvard Business Review*, May 1963. Accessed May 19, 2018. https://hbr.org/1963/05/managing-for-business-effectiveness.
2 Masaaki Imai, *Gemba Kaizen* (McGraw-Hill, 2012) 149.
3 Anthony Manos and Chad Vincent, Editors, *The Lean Handbook* (ASQ Quality Press, Milwaukee, WI, 2012) 59.
4 Masaaki Imai, *Gemba Kaizen* (McGraw-Hill, 2012) 149.
5 Recognition to the members of the Moodle Oversight Team for their vision and commitment in the development of a statewide learning management system, November 18, 2015.
6 Bill Gates, as quoted by 2013 Lean Systems Summit. The Lean Collaborative, Portland Maine.
7 Ohio Department of Administrative Services. Innovate Before You Automate (2015). LeanOhio.gov http://lean.ohio.gov/Portals/0/docs/info/LeanOhio_Innovate_Before_You_Automate_july2015.pdf.
8 Masaaki Imai, *Gemba Kaizen* (McGraw-Hill: 2012) 227–228.

6

Six Sigma vs. Six Signatures and Six Weeks

Lean is often linked with a related discipline, Six Sigma. As the practice of Lean has developed, credentialing programs are increasingly available in Lean, and in Lean-Six Sigma. It's useful to understand the distinction and application of the highly structured statistical approach of Six Sigma and the low-tech Lean techniques we use in our public-sector work. Dagmar Vlahos, Lean Coordinator for the University of New Hampshire, was credentialed in Six Sigma in a previous private sector job. Dagmar regularly briefs participants in BET's Lean Black Belt program on the distinction between Lean and Six Sigma. We make it clear to our program participants that they are not receiving a Six Sigma credential, but that they should be familiar with the discipline.

Originally developed by Motorola and Allied Signal and refined by General Electric, the structured methodology is particularly useful in reducing defects and variation in manufacturing and it can be applied to other fields. DES Lean practitioner Tom Guertin explains that the Six Sigma refers to six times the standard deviation (6σ or $\pm 3\sigma$). To achieve the Six Sigma quality metric, the process would produce only 3.4 defects per million opportunities. The measurement-based approach focuses on process improvement and variation reduction through the application of Six Sigma improvement projects. Unnecessary variation in a process can result in significant delays and poor quality of decisions and outputs. The Six Sigma method of Define, Measure, Analyze, Improve, Control (DMAIC) is a system for continuously improving existing processes that fall below specifications."[1]

In *The Lean Toolbox*, DMAIC is explained as a version of Plan–Do–Check–Act/Adjust (PDCA), with an expanded use of the "Plan" phase, noting, "Lean sets the philosophical background of value-focused thinking ... Six Sigma—as a tool for variability reduction and tough problem clarification fits very well into the wider umbrella of Lean."[2] The structure of DMAIC, with tollgate checks in between phases, requires a level of precision and focus that can be helpful in major projects using data to demonstrate potential return on investment. The extended planning and data gathering phase is not necessary for every Lean project, but it is useful for advanced Lean practitioners to understand and to adapt as part of their toolbox.

Lean and Six Sigma coexist. Our Lean work is to build a culture of continuous improvement, seeking to maximize value to our customers. It is more fundamental and comprehensive than a series of formal, structured events. The DMAIC approach can be used to transform elaborate processes, and Lean practitioners can adapt the disciplined metric based method to enhance our low-tech approach.

We realize the value of a hybrid approach, particularly concerning metrics. When were first started, there was so much *muda* in our bureaucracies, we didn't use precise measurements. Improvement opportunities were plentiful, and the Lean tools were easy to use. We happily saved days, weeks, or even months, by redesigning our work processes. We didn't spend much time quantifying it.

METRICS VS. "IT'S MUCH BETTER"

If there's an opportunity to lean a process, it's tempting just to go for it, rather than waiting to develop baseline metrics. This is especially true when we were recruiting project teams for Yellow Belt classes—we didn't want to create barriers to enrollment by assigning pre-work. Due to the prevalent *muri*, and lack of management commitment, it was difficult enough to find work teams with the time available to attend a 3-day program, without adding the expectation that they would arrive with metrics on the current state.

A slide in the State of Washington's "Introduction to Lean Thinking" video explains, "Lean is about incremental improvement. 30% now instead of 100% later ... or never. By the time we've perfectly planned a 100% improvement we've lost valuable time and the business environment will have changed."[3]

In retrospect, however, we should have standardized some rudimentary metrics. Our early projects resulted in processes that were described as "so much better." We often had no idea how much better they were because we had never measured them before. As the Lean program matured, we realized the importance of documenting the gains. A lack of consistent metrics impeded the ability to compile data. It was difficult to aggregate gains in a dozen departments, spanning nearly a decade. Despite some great case studies, we fell short on the overall "so-what?" factor.

As Dr. Deming said, "In God we trust; all others must bring data."[4] On the other hand, excess information is a form of waste. Bert Teeuwen cautions, "Data essentially has no value unless it can be converted into usable information."[5] We need to focus our data collection to provide the information required to improve our processes that enable us to accomplish our mission.

Let's examine how the use of work time and cycle time can illustrate *muda* and support the case for making change. Using the out-of-state travel permission process "six signatures in six weeks," we'll work through a sample *kaizen* that captures typical work time and cycle time.

THE OUT-OF-STATE TRAVEL PROCESS AS A HYPOTHETICAL PROJECT

The six signatures in this chapter's title refer to a stubbornly entrenched process that requires as many as six signatures for permission to travel out-of-state. The cumbersome requirements are the same for permission to fly across the country or to drive a car to a neighboring New England state. Though the actual number of signatures varies depending on the rank of the prospective traveler within the bureaucracy, six is the number typically required at DHHS.

A classic example of bureaucratic *muda*, as described in Chapter 5, this process is also the basis for a hypothetical scenario used in Lean Yellow Belt classes. Although it is preferable for Yellow Belt students to bring real workplace projects for the hands-on section of the training, this scenario can be used as an alternative project. Students who don't work in this type of bureaucracy have trouble believing that something this bizarre exists. It's good practice as a *kaizen* exercise.

Since it's not a real project, the participants don't have information about the amount of time it takes for all travel requests; they are asked to map a single scenario that will illustrate the problem. Consider the following summary table:

	Current State	Future State
Total work time	80 minutes	40 minutes
Total cycle time	6 weeks = 225 hours	1 hour

Current state work time. Complete the form = 30 minutes; next 5 signers to review and sign = 10 minutes × 5 signers = 50 minutes. Total work time = 80 minutes.

Current state cycle time to get through the six signatures = 6 weeks; 5 work days per week = 30 days; 7.5 hours per day = 225 hours.

Future state work time. Complete the form = 30 minutes; supervisor reviews and signs = 10 minutes. Total work time = 40 minutes.

Future state cycle time to complete the form; send it to the supervisor to complete a review and sign it = 1 hour.

The project team members understand that they don't have a real sponsor, so their sell will be made to someone playing the role of the commissioner. Since it's not a real project, the changes they propose will not be implemented, but they can calculate the amount of time that could be saved. It's also a good lesson about the key role for the sponsor in Lean events.

Learning objectives for a hypothetical project on out-of-state travel:

- To apply Lean tools of process mapping and the 5 Whys
- To recognize and reduce the wastes of waiting and under-utilized human talent
- To apply the Lean principles of aligning authority and responsibility at the lowest possible level

Debrief after the role-play

- Ask the participants why they think the process is so entrenched.

- Discuss the principles of good process design, mistake-proofing, and alignment of authority and responsibility. What kind of cultural change would be required? What training?
- Share a quote from *The Lean Handbook*, "the most effective way to maximize resources is to ensure that quality (as defined by your customer) is built in...by the people doing the work...It has also been proven many times that even 100% inspection is only 80%–90% effective. Quality at the source involves a cultural change."[6]

The draft charter, roles, and instructions for the *kaizen* event are in Appendix B.

LEAN TOOLS FOR ANALYSIS

It's worth noting that many of the techniques categorized as Lean tools were developed long before the term "lean" was coined. They fit perfectly, however, into the discipline of Lean because of the foundational Plan–Do–Check (or Study)–Act/Adjust cycle. Using the PDCA/PDSA approach, practitioners can focus on the actual rather than assumed causes of the problem, enabling them to develop more effective solutions. Remember, even with a clear understanding of the root cause, the "check," "study," and "adjust" steps are critical to control for unintended negative consequences.

Those new to Lean are quick to propose solutions without understanding the reason the process has grown its *muda*. Facilitators understand this tendency and guide their teams to capture their "bright ideas" without allowing them to be incorporated immediately into a project. Before designing the future state, teams need to understand why the process is conducted as it is in the current state.

Process thinking takes practice. Don't accept "culture" as an excuse; use the 5 Whys to figure out what's going on. It's tempting for rookies to cast blame on coworkers. In *The Lean Toolbox*, we're reminded that blaming people is not an acceptable response as a root cause. Remember Deming's 94/6 rule—"Most of the problems lie with the system or the process, not the people."[7]

Once the root cause has been found, dig deeper. If the team already knows that there is a better way to do it, why hasn't it changed? Identify the barriers to change. Is there a problem that prevents a better way of doing it? If so, why hasn't that problem been solved? What countermeasures would be required to solve it?

Our New Hampshire Lean program was slow to introduce some of the tools, and 8 years into the program, we're playing catch-up. I was reassured to see Bert Teeuwen's advice that it's okay to "save the sophisticated tools for later." He explains, "A start made with simple tools can yield considerable gain in the first few years … It's like picking apples from a tree. The low-hanging fruit is easy to pick without advanced instruments. The higher the fruit, the more instruments one needs."[8]

The basic tools are not difficult to use, even by someone math-phobic like me, but I needed some coaching to get started. I mention my slow start both to acknowledge colleagues like Justin Kenney and Tyler Brandow who assisted me, and to have it serve as a reminder that we need a broad bench of talent in our Lean endeavors.

There are many more tools than those covered in this section. For example, *The Lean Six Sigma Pocket Toolbook* is a quick reference guide for nearly 100 tools.[9] We'll be discussing a few of them, along with a couple of examples of how they can be applied in *kaizens* common to public sector business processes.

Commonly used tools include Pareto charts, 5 Why worksheets, fishbone diagrams, A3 templates, and SIPOCs. This section covers the use of Pareto charts, fishbone diagrams and SIPOCs. Examples of A3 templates and 5 Whys are provided in Chapter 8.

PARETO CHARTS

The "80/20 rule" is based on work by economist and sociologist Vilfredo Pareto, who found that around 80% of the wealth was held by about 20% of the people. Dr. Joseph Juran subsequently applied this concept to management. The Pareto principle states that, for many events, roughly 80% of the effects come from 20% of the causes.

Pareto charts combine a bar chart with a line graph to identify the "vital few"—the roughly 20% of factors which cause 80% of the problems.

Lacking this analysis, teams may focus on anecdotal perceptions of the problem, failing to adopt appropriate countermeasures for the most significant factors. The following section uses a call center as an example to illustrate the use of a Pareto chart. The instructions are based on guidance from *The Lean Handbook*.[10]

Pareto Chart Example

A team working to reduce the number of calls to the DHHS call center needs to identify the primary causes for their calls. Since complaint calls are generally the most difficult to handle, the team is eager to brainstorm about how to reduce those calls. The team leader wants to make sure their efforts are focused on the most common problems, so she asks them to collect data prior to the Lean event.

> Step 1: Collect information on the number of calls, and the various reasons for the calls.
>
> Step 2: Sort the reasons into categories and count the number of times each was reported.
>
> Step 3: Using a table format, list the most frequently reported circumstances at the top, descending to the least common.

Reason for Calls	Number of Calls
Seeking reinstatement of claim denied due to missing information	12
Seeking reinstatement of claim denied due to clerical error by case worker	7
Calling wrong agency—a program that's not in our jurisdiction	6
Updating information on status—change in income, address, etc.	5
Calling to clarify eligibility requirements	3
Calling to complain about case worker rudeness	3

> Step 4. Cumulative Count: starting with the top category, populate the column of Cumulative Count with a running total of occurrences, with the total at the bottom of the table
>
> Step 5. Individual Percentage—populate the Individual Percentage column with the number of occurrences in each category divided by the total number of occurrences. Ex: there were 12 calls requesting reinstatement of claims denied due to missing information. 12 divided by 36 = 0.33

Reason for Calls	Number of Calls	Cumulative Count	Individual%	Cumulative%
Seeking reinstatement of claim denied due to missing information	12	12	33.3	
Seeking reinstatement of claim denied due to clerical error by case worker	7	19	19.4	
Called the wrong agency— not in our jurisdiction	6	25	16.6	
Called to update information— address, income, etc.	5	30	13.8	
Calling to clarify eligibility requirements	3	33	8.3	
Calling to complain about case worker rudeness	3	36	8.3	

Step 6. Cumulative percentage—start at the top of the chart—the cumulative percentage of the first category is the same as its cumulative percentage. The cumulative for the second item is the sum of the first two, and so on. The total cumulative percentage should equal 100%.

Reason for Calls	Number of Calls	Cumulative Count	Individual%	Cumulative%
Seeking reinstatement of claim denied due to missing information	12	12	33.3	33.3
Seeking reinstatement of claim denied due to clerical error by case worker	7	19	19.4	52.7
Called the wrong agency— not in our jurisdiction	6	25	16.6	69.3
Called to update information—address, income, etc.	5	30	13.8	83.1
Calling to clarify eligibility requirements	3	33	8.3	91.4
Calling to complain about case worker rudeness	3	36	8.3	100

Instructions for Creating the Chart

- The horizontal axis represents categories. List the items from the data table along the horizontal access, starting with the most frequently occurring items on the left.
- Draw two vertical axes. The left axis is Frequency (use increments totaling the highest frequency category) and the right axis is Percent, in increments up to 100.
- Draw the bars so the height of each bar corresponds to the frequency of occurrences in that category.
- Place a dot on the chart indicating the cumulative percentage for each category. Connect the dots with a line showing the progression of the cumulative percentage up to the 100% mark on the right axis.

Using the call center data as an example, the Pareto chart below can help the Lean team to focus on the primary reasons people are calling. The trend line across the chart shows that most of the calls are generated for three reasons. If relying solely on anecdotal information, the team might have focused on how they could reduce complaints (Figure 6.1).

Using the Pareto chart, the call center team learned that most of calls were related to missing or erroneously entered information. Now, they'll use a fishbone diagram to trace the root causes of the primary cause: missing or faulty information. The "fishbone" cause and effect diagram was originally created by Kaoru Ishikawa, a Japanese professor of engineering, so it is also known as the Ishikawa diagram.

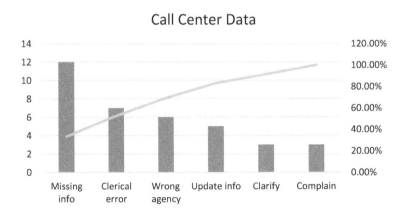

FIGURE 6.1
Sample Pareto chart using call center data.

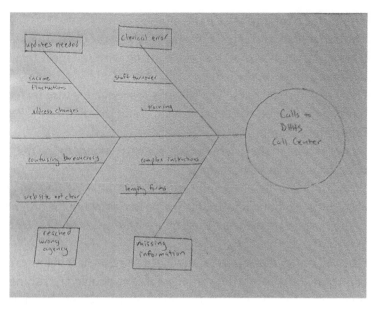

FIGURE 6.2
Sample fishbone diagram.

- Write, "Calls to DHHS Call Center" in the head of the fish.
- Label the fishbone headings with the primary causes.
- Brainstorm contributing causes under each category and list them on the fish bones

For example, under the cause of "missing information," the team might list "lengthy forms" or "complex instructions" as contributing factors. Based on those identified factors, the team might propose simplifying the forms (Figure 6.2).

SUPPLIERS-INPUTS-PROCESS-OUTPUTS-CUSTOMER (SIPOC)

A SIPOC is a high-level chart that can be used as a first step in understanding a process, prior to process mapping. Its structured format shows the sequence of transactions and dependencies. According to *The Lean Handbook*, the SIPOC shows that "nothing in the organization is done in isolation. In one way or another, everyone serves either the customer or someone else who does."[11]

- Suppliers: The people or organizations that provide information, material, and resources to be worked on in the process.
- Inputs: The information/materials provided by suppliers that are transformed by the process.
- Process: The series of steps that transform the inputs.
- Outputs: The product or service used by the customer.
- Customer: The people, organization, or another process that receives the output from the process.

Instructions: Some practitioners recommend starting with the Process (1), moving to Outputs (2), then Customer (3), back to Inputs (4), and then Suppliers (5). Others use a traditional left to right approach to complete the SIPOC.

In the example below, the employee requesting permission to travel is the Supplier of the A-24 form, and is also the end-user customer of the form, once the process is completed. The SIPOC of the six signatures (employee—supervisor—bureau chief—finance director—division director—commissioner) can be constructed prior to mapping the workflow.

5	4	1	2	3
Suppliers	**Inputs**	**Process**	**Outputs**	**Customer**
Employee	A-24 form	Review by Supervisor	Signature of Supervisor	Bureau Chief
Supervisor	A-24 form signed by Supervisor	Review by Bureau Chief	Signature of Bureau Chief	Finance Director
Bureau Chief	A-24 signed by Bureau Chief	Review by Finance Director	Signature of Finance Director	Division Director
Finance Director	A-24 signed by Finance Director	Review by Division Director	Signature of Division Director	Commissioner
Division Director	A-24 signed by Division Director	Review by Commissioner	Signature of Commissioner	**Employee**

SUMMARY OF LESSONS LEARNED

Lesson #1—Metrics matter. Even if we're not measuring in Six Sigma level specificity, Lean practitioners should be documenting the time it takes to conduct our work processes to establish a baseline for measuring improvements once the process change is implemented.

- Our toolbox was too light. Our Yellow Belt training focused primarily on process mapping, and our Green Belt training prepared facilitators to lead *kaizen* mapping events. We've added continuing education workshops and posted materials in online classrooms, but that's not a substitute for an integrated approach. Vermont's Lean training program integrates tool use at every belt level.

- The formal DMAIC structure of Six Sigma is useful to understand. The focus on reduction in variation and in defects underscores the importance of standard work. While our Lean work encourages informal "just do it" events and *kaizens* of simple processes, Lean practitioners should be familiar with a range of advanced techniques.

Lesson #2—Don't try to prove Lean's worth by boasting about cost savings. That will give the false impression that Lean is a cost-cutting program, rather than a management system.

Lesson #3—Metrics can be persuasive, but just because it's measurable doesn't make it meaningful.

How will you collect the measurements that matter? What documentation might persuade management to reduce the six signatures required for permission to travel?

- It takes only seconds to sign your name. How do you document wasted time?

- How would you collect data on the increased cost of airline ticket prices, late conference registration fees or hotel costs?

Lesson #4—Root cause analysis can be revelatory. Use the 5 Whys and/ or the fishbone diagram to understand how certain aspects of the process developed, and identify the barriers to improvement before designing the new workflow.

Lesson #5—Use the PDCA cycle to understand each current condition. Mike Rother, whose *Toyota Kata* is required reading for New Hampshire's Black Belts, links scientific thinking and deliberative practice. Rother's Kata model uses short cycles of experiments toward each new target condition. He cautions against "Pareto paralysis," noting that "by the time we decided what the biggest problem was, the situation at the process had changed."[12]

APPLYING THE LESSONS

- Learn a variety of tools and practice using them. Integrate the tools throughout the Lean training programs. The goal is problem solving, not the application of any specific tool. With deliberative practice, proficient use of tools will become a natural part of your PDCA cycle.
- Build a broad and deep bench of practitioners. The culture of continuous improvement requires activities at all levels of the organization from "just do it" to formally chartered *kaizens* to complex DMAIC projects.

Measurement is not a "set-it and forget it" task. Metrics are needed to confirm that the improvements worked as expected, and to assure the *muda* doesn't return. Pay attention to the Check and Adjust components of the PDCA cycle.

NOTES

1 "Variation in Government Processes," Tom Guertin, March 2018 (unpublished), and EPA Lean in Government Improvement Methods. Accessed April 5, 2018. www.epa.gov/lean/lean-and-six-sigma-process-improvement-methods.
2 John Bicheno and Matthias Holweg, *The Lean Toolbox 5th Edition* (Picsie Books, 2016) 99.
3 "Introduction to Lean Thinking," State of Washington. www.youtube.com/watch?v=RxDw0Q_gVt0.
4 The W. Edwards Deming Institute. W. Edwards Deming Quotes. Accessed May 15, 2018. http://quotes.deming.org/category/data.
5 Bert Teeuwen, *Lean for the Public Sector: The Pursuit of Perfection in Public Service* (Taylor & Francis Group, LLC, Productivity Press, New York, 2011) 101.
6 Anthony Manos and Chad Vincent, Editors, *The Lean Handbook* (ASQ Quality Press, Milwaukee, WI, 2012) 71.
7 John Bicheno and Matthias Holweg, *The Lean Toolbox 5th Edition* (Picsie Books, 2016) 55.

8 Bert Teeuwen, *Lean for the Public Sector: The Pursuit of Perfection in Public Service* (Taylor & Francis Group, LLC, Productivity Press, New York, 2011) 53–54.

9 Michael L. George and David Rowland, et al. *The Lean Six Sigma Pocket Toolbook* (McGraw-Hill, 2005).

10 Anthony Manos and Chad Vincent, Editors, *The Lean Handbook* (ASQ Quality Press, Milwaukee, WI, 2012) 190–193.

11 Anthony Manos and Chad Vincent, Editors, *The Lean Handbook* (ASQ Quality Press, Milwaukee, WI, 2012) 155.

12 Mike Rother, *Toyota Kata* (McGraw-Hill Education, 2010) 124.

7

Lean for Leaders

This chapter is divided into three sections. It begins with a discussion of entrenched bureaucratic dysfunction. Next, it covers the content of a "Lean for Leaders" workshop for administrators. While focusing on the role of top management, the workshop identifies the responsibilities of staff at all levels in the organization during a Lean initiative. The chapter closes with strategies needed to launch a sustainable Lean program.

BUREAUCRAZY

New Hampshire's Lean practitioners have always faced an uphill battle to remove monuments of bureaucratic red tape. In 2008, the Pew report[1] acknowledged the dynamic tension between control and managerial flexibility, while observing that "New Hampshire is at the extreme of the control spectrum." In 2015, Governor Hassan's Innovation Commission observed, "The problem is not with the people, but rather with processes and an environment that places control above all else, even good or common sense."[2]

In *The Lean Toolbox*, the authors stress the significance of management involvement, noting that "It is difficult to think of a successful Lean transformation that has not had real commitment and involvement from the top."[3]

Former BET Director Dennis Martino commented on the organizational psychology and power dynamics that can either facilitate or cripple Lean initiatives:

> Most bottlenecks occur when managers in the chain of command are threatened by change. Or they tamp down change to exert control and by

doing so accentuate their power. I call this the "Martinet effect." It is based on the observation that some mid-level managers exert authority because they can. The way to do that is to control everything.

The way around this phenomenon starts at the very top. In New Hampshire, success was highest and most pronounced in agencies where the commissioner set the clear direction and established protocols and nomination processes to assure monthly improvement projects. Or the commissioner was a cheerleader for change and really recognized and praised process improvement efforts. In both cases a cultural change resulted.

The Department of Safety is the best example of the former type, clear direction. The commissioner, John Barthelmes, laid out orders that projects would be nominated and for how projects would be scheduled. Safety is an example of a paramilitary organization where orders from the top are not challenged by middle management. Lean projects became the routine. Employees were recognized and praised for their efforts.

Lean practitioners are dealing with two issues—a lack of understanding of Lean and a lack of agreement. It was not always evident which was which, and if the two were interwoven. As one administrator observed, "The life of a petty bureaucrat is hoard, hold, and hide." Many of them have learned to wait for things to go away, with the attitude of "they're going to have to come find me, and there are too many of us." Another Lean practitioner warned, "We must not underestimate the power of an experienced bureaucrat to passively resist."

As a practical matter, Lean practitioners must deal with the challenge. Middle managers opt out of Lean projects because their employees are too busy to participate. If projects do occur, they can postpone implementation indefinitely, due to more urgent priorities. Given the persistent *muri*, we know that these are both valid reasons—we are too busy, and we always have urgent priorities. All managers are responsible for operations, but few are held responsible for improving systems. If upper management never articulated system improvement as an organizational priority, or assigned it as part of the job, are mid-level managers resistant or realistic?

While acknowledging the most frequently cited cause for stalled Lean initiatives is middle management resistance, Jim Womack explains that "the root cause of regression...is confusion about priorities at different levels of the organization, compounded by the failure to make anyone responsible for the continuing performance of important value streams as they flow horizontally across the enterprise."[4] The alignment of authority and responsibility at appropriate levels is facilitated by clarity of expectations for operational excellence.

The Shingo Institute outlines a multidimensional model, explaining "Operational excellence cannot be a program, another new set of tools or a new management fad. Operational excellence is the consequence of an enterprise-wide practice of ideal behaviors based on correct principles. As long as improvement is seen as something outside the core work of the business, as long as it is viewed as "something else to do," operational excellence will remain elusive."[5]

We can't expect administrators with successful careers based on decades of experience, with advanced degrees in traditional management to suddenly become Lean managers. Perhaps they've heard good things about Lean projects and they're willing to try it out. If they are open to learning more, we can present a workshop to help them integrate the process improvement techniques within the overarching frame of Lean management.

LEAN FOR LEADERS WORKSHOP

The workshop runs 60–90 minutes and has five parts: overview of Lean, roles and responsibilities in a Lean organization, the manager's role in chartering and sponsoring Lean projects, Lean management, and moving forward with Lean in state government and in your agency.

The learning objectives are

- To be able to lead an organization in a Lean initiative, understanding your role and that of your managers, supervisors, employees and Lean practitioners.
- To select and prioritize Lean projects that align with agency strategic priorities, and identify managers who will be responsible for chartering those projects
- To understand that Lean is more than just a process improvement tool, and to examine the concept of Lean management.

Before starting the workshop, give the participants a quick 3-minute warm-up (for their reference later in the program, not to be turned in).

- At work, I would love to spend more time on ___ if only I could spend less time on ___.
- "Of all the processes in my organization _____ is the most challenging/troublesome/aggravating." Examples: hiring, purchasing, reclassifications.

PART I: OVERVIEW OF LEAN

Instructions to trainer: use a condensed version of the introductory material from the Yellow Belt class (in Chapter 2) to describe Lean (5–10 minutes, max). Consider the definition:

> Lean is an organizational performance management system characterized by a collaborative approach between employees and managers to identify and minimize or eliminate activities that do not create value for the customers of a business process, or stakeholders.[6]

PART II: ROLES AND RESPONSIBILITIES IN A LEAN ORGANIZATION

Roles for Leaders

Leaders identify strategic priorities, and articulate organizational goals. Lean activities should be conducted that support the achievement of those goals by improving the priority processes, and by leaning sub-processes so that staff can be redeployed away from low priority tasks.

In launching a Lean initiative, leaders must assure access to training, so that people are properly prepared to understand their new responsibilities. Leaders must also communicate a firm commitment that Lean is not about cutting staff. At the Department of Safety, for example, jobs may change due to a Lean project, but staff will not lose their livelihoods. Recall Deming said, "Drive out fear, so that everyone may work effectively for the company."[7]

Throughout the Lean initiative, leaders are responsible for assuring that process owners (managers) sponsor *kaizen* events, assign project teams, and set timelines for implementation of the improvements.

Leaders create a sustainable Lean culture by aligning responsibility and authority at the lowest possible level, communicating results and praising progress.

Exercise #1: Purpose and Process

- Identify the top three strategic priorities of your organization
- What prevents you from accomplishing them?
- How difficult is it to do basic things? Sample performance metrics:
  - On average, how long does it take your department to hire someone from vacancy to establishment of start date?
  - On average, how long does it take your department to complete a contract from RFP to establishment of a vendor start date?

Roles for Managers

Managers sponsor *kaizen* events to lean the processes in their areas of responsibility. They may also co-sponsor events with managers from other sections to deal with processes that cross organizational silos. The events are developed by working with Lean practitioners on charters with measurable goals and assigning the right teams. (More about this later in the session.)

Managers authorize the implementation of changes recommended by the *kaizen* teams, and assure changes are implemented. They are responsible for documenting the metrics before and after the event, assuring that the gains are sustained, and modifying the changes, as appropriate (PDCA).

Managers should take an introduction to Lean class—some organizations offer a White Belt program (generally 2–3 hours). It is useful for managers to understand the techniques used in a basic *kaizen* such as process mapping, as well as key Lean principles.

Roles for Employees

Employees at all ranks should take an introduction to Lean class, preparing them to be active participants in the organization's Lean initiative.

Employees participate in Lean project teams and identify opportunities for large- and small-scale *kaizen* events.

Employees build Lean culture by spreading the word about successful projects. As Lean culture develops, employees will apply 5S and "just do it" continuous improvement principles to their daily work.

Employees who are enthusiastic about Lean should consider becoming Lean practitioners. Management should be on the look-out for these folks who have been "bitten by the Lean bug," and make sure that they have opportunities to continue their training.

Roles for Lean Practitioners

Lean practitioners work with managers to prepare charters with measurable goals, schedule Lean events, and assign the right teams. They facilitate *kaizen* events, guiding the participants to redesign processes prioritizing customer value, congruent with Lean principles.

These practitioners build Lean capacity by identifying opportunities to use *kaizen* and other Lean tools, and mentor new Lean practitioners. They may acquire advanced skills in Lean and assist in organizational transformation.

Exercise #2: List Your Top Two Priority Projects

Considerations may include:

- Degree of criticality to agency
- Administrative bottlenecks
- Customer complaints
- Need to comply with federal standards
- Staff interest, opportunity to build morale and develop Lean capacity
- "Biggest bang for our buck" projects that would benefit multiple divisions
- Feasibility

PART III: MANAGER'S ROLE IN SPONSORING *KAIZEN* EVENTS

Kaizen means "change for the better" and a *kaizen* event is a facilitated, small-scope improvement activity that engages the creativity of employees to reduce waste in a work process. *Kaizen* events typically run 3-5 days.

Select the right sponsor: The manager sponsoring the event should have the authority to approve a redesign of the process workflow. He/she authorizes the work to be undertaken by the team and empowers the team to redesign the process. Note: More than one sponsor may be required for events that cross jurisdictional lines, or if the recommended improvements require approval from higher ranks within the organization.

Prior to the event, the sponsor works with the Lean facilitator to develop the draft charter. The charter document should identify specific improvement goals, linked to measurable results. It is optimal if the sponsor knows the current "baseline" metrics or can gather that data prior to the event.

Examples of goals for process improvement:

- Reduce the number of applications returned for re-work from _____ to _____.
- Decrease the amount of time to issue a permit to a qualified applicant from _____ to _____.

The sponsor is responsible for assigning the right team. It is essential to include employees who work in all sections of the process, so they can examine the process from start to finish. This may require coordinating with a manager from another department, rescheduling other tasks, or finding coverage. Be sure to include front-line administrative staff—if they're part of the process, they need to be on the team. Don't omit people you expect to be resistant to change. It's important to include them for the knowledge they bring and for the role they need to play in the actual implementation of the improvement.

While the charter is a living document, subject to revision during the event, the sponsor should identify the scope and parameters of the project. Examples of guidance to the team: Improve the process using existing staff (no new positions); IT staff will be provided to assist the team for a maximum of 2 hours. The team is encouraged to focus on improvements within their own division, and broader issues will be dealt with in subsequent *kaizen* events.

During the *kaizen* event, the sponsor should be available to consult with the facilitator to provide guidance, if requested. Items for consultation could include: approving project scope change, if appropriate; removing obstacles; or identifying subject matter experts, such as IT staff, to consult with the team.

PART IV: LEAN MANAGEMENT

Instructions to the trainer: Below are a series of discussion points for examining the superhero models of leadership and transitioning to a discussion of Lean management.

Consider the belief system that the top job requires super smart, super dedicated, super responsible people—implied in the term "super"-vision. The organization's survival relies on you. No one else shares your level of commitment or competence. You must come up with all the answers and solve every problem.

Discuss firefighting metaphors. There's an adrenaline rush in emergency response. Reacting to continual crises can become an ego-centric habit. You are indispensable in solving the daily crisis. The approach can be exhilarating. It's not as interesting as engaging a team in disciplined, sustained problem solving.

Flip the firefighting analogy: real firefighting involves much more than running into burning buildings. Training and drilling with the proper equipment prepares the team for success when a crisis occurs. Understanding the root causes of fire hazards and developing appropriate countermeasures can prevent crises from occurring.

Womack explains that organizations are over-led and under-managed—we're obsessed with leadership while ignoring the need for management. Lean management explains why the idealized view of charismatic leadership—looking for the next "great leader" to save the organization falls short. It ignores the need to manage differently.

Lean management is both a top-down and a bottom-up system. Leaders articulate the mission and identify the priorities. Responsibility and authority is placed at the lowest possible level, where work is taking place at the *gemba*. Recall Toyota's success in empowering workers on the assembly line to use the Andon cord to deal with defects.

Leaders shouldn't assume that employee empowerment relieves them of their responsibility to articulate the mission. Purpose comes first. As Womack explained, "engaging in the problem-solving process is actually the highest form of respect."[8]

Jim Lancaster, CEO of Lantech, describes moving the management style from traditional to transformational: "I have always had a problem convincing CEOs of one simple thing...to take the time to go where value is actually created. They need to learn to see the work and to see how their management system utterly fails to support the daily work."[9] *The Lean Handbook* explains that *gemba* walks are now standard work for leaders.

The transition to a Lean organization requires a shift from an authority-based to a responsibility-based organization.

Management must shift focus from a debate about who owns what (authority) to a dialog around what is the right thing to do (responsibility).

Lean managers avoid relying on their authority to instruct others, striving whenever possible to lead by influence and example, as if they have no authority.

Traditional Management vs. Lean Management—Quiz #1

What number of signatures is required to attend a fully funded, professionally appropriate conference?

   a. None—verbal permission from your supervisor
   b. One—your supervisor
   c. Two to three
   d. Four or more

Debrief: If more than one signature is required, explain the rationale.

Traditional Management vs. Lean Management—Quiz #2

What level of approval is required for managers to purchase necessary equipment and hire essential personnel already in his/her budget?

   a. None—consult if you have questions; do all hiring and purchasing with quality and efficiency
   b. Administrator and/or department head
   c. A committee appointed by the department head
   d. The governor's office
   e. B–D

Debrief: Explain the rationale for managers not having authority to purchase items already in their budgets.

Following the quizzes, we revisit the definition of management. According to Mike Rother, it's "the systematic pursuit of desired conditions by utilizing human capabilities in a concerted way."[10]

The Shingo Institute in the Jon S. Huntsman School of Business at Utah State University is an excellent resource. The Institute's work is based on the work of Dr. Shigeo Shingo. As noted in the Shingo Model, "One of Dr. Shingo's little known, but perhaps most important, contributions was his understanding of the relationship between concepts (principles), systems and tools."[11] The Shingo model is studied in advanced Lean courses and quotes from Dr. Shingo are used throughout the belt program to illustrate the key concepts.

Below are three quotes that provide useful insights:

> The primary role of a leader is to drive the principles of operational excellence into the culture.
>
> The primary role of managers must shift from firefighting to designing, aligning, and improving systems.
>
> The more deeply leaders, managers and associates understand the principles of operational excellence and the more perfectly systems are aligned to reinforce ideal behavior, the greater the probability of creating a sustainable culture of excellence where achieving ideal results is the norm rather than the aspiration.[12]

> *Shigeo Shingo, 1909–1990 Industrial Engineer, Toyota*

Questions for discussion

- How do you align appropriate authority with responsibility?
- How can you articulate your values for excellence in public service?
- How can you develop trust in your managers, supervisors, and employees to carry out the organization's mission?

Examine the root causes of the *muda* of multiple layers of checking. Consider the elements of trust, competency, and character. Could those who have been trained in traditional management learn to build an organization where employees have the responsibility to stop the assembly line, to make decisions about attending conferences, purchasing products? What level of checking is appropriate? Sam McKeeman observed that you can't have someone you don't trust stopping the line at Toyota. He noted that as trust goes up, the cost of doing business goes down, and productivity goes up. You build a trusting culture with people who are competent and of good character—hire good people, train them well, get out of the way.

Consider using the "5 Whys" to understand legacy systems. Asking "why" five times can drill down toward the root cause of a problem. For example:

Problem: Vendors are charging late fees on our invoices. Why? We can't pay them in the 30-day period required. Why? The accounting department sends payment at the end of each month. Why? The department heads are frequently late in forwarding the invoices to accounting. Why? The department heads need to check with the frontline supervisors to confirm that the product was received. Why?

This chain of reasoning could lead a manager to charter a *kaizen* event, assigning a team of staff from accounting and other departments to design a new workflow for the accounts payable process. The *kaizen* team could drill down further into the root cause by asking "why" again: Why do department heads sign invoices? The answer could be that a frontline supervisor once bought something unauthorized or inappropriate.

A single mistake or malfeasance by one employee, one time, may have resulted in additional process requirements. The Lean team should consider methods to mistake-proof the process, other than using a "hard stop" on every invoice by requiring a department head's signature. They could propose spot-checking or other techniques to screen for errors or dishonesty. What is the optimal design of checks and balances for fiduciary stewardship? How can a process be built for efficiency and integrity?

Exercise: Managing the Processes

How do you define process excellence? List the primary processes used in your organization and rate them according to your criteria for excellence. How do you think they rate from the perspective of the front-line employees? From the customers' perspective?

Managing by process: Review lessons from Jim Womack's *Gemba Walks* on traditional ("modern") management compared to Lean management. Modern management focuses on vertical functions and departments in the organization as mechanisms of optimization and control. Most enterprises are organized vertically, with each department functioning as its own silo as it interacts with other departments.

Lean management focuses on horizontal flow of value across many organizations, from raw materials to the end use customer. Lean tools are needed to cross the silos to maximize the quality and flow of the product or service to the customer. As Jim Womack explained in *Gemba Walks*, enterprises are organized vertically, while the flow of value to the customer is horizontal across the organization.[13] The charts below illustrate an example of horizontal structure and vertical process flow (Figures 7.1 and 7.2).

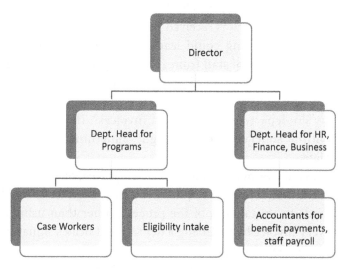

FIGURE 7.1
Vertical organizational structure.

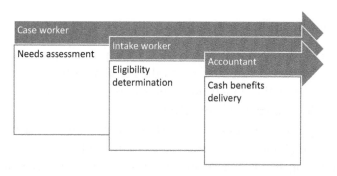

FIGURE 7.2
Horizontal flow of value to the customer.

PART V: MOVING FORWARD WITH LEAN

Discussion of concerns and challenges.

Generate a list of barriers you anticipate. What concerns do you have? Consider the following:

- If employees are empowered to redesign their own work processes, is there a risk that they will set it up for their own convenience, rather than the public? How do you embed the Lean concept of value for the customer?
- Will there be blowback for requiring bureau chiefs or department heads to work across their silos? Will they refuse to allow employees to redesign the work processes? How will you hold them accountable?
- So many positions have been lost, the staff is completely overloaded— we'll never get the required work done if they stop their daily tasks for Lean training and *kaizen* projects. *Muri* is real. How will you address it?

Exercise: You're the Sponsor

There are a series of components to build Lean capacity: Conduct projects, assure follow-through, identify change agents, train facilitators, document gains, and celebrate successes.

Start by identifying a few potential projects. Return to the list they generated earlier in the workshop for ideas. Other considerations for project selection: Are employees chasing information? Waiting for approvals? Constantly getting interrupted? Is work getting lost between department silos? What is the customer experience? Is there a backlog of work?

Start with some small-scale projects, then move to the consequential. What processes are most critical to your agency's strategic goals? What processes occupy most of your employees' time now?

Instructions:

- Select a project to sponsor.
- Sketch out a draft charter and draft a problem statement, with specific management goals.
- Identify the customer.

- Consider roles for the project manager and team members. Remember to include employees from each section that touches the process.
- Save the draft charter from this workshop to incorporate into your Lean initiative.

Launching your Lean Initiative

- Review your notes from earlier in the workshop. Summarize your top priorities and identify the organizational processes needed to accomplish those priorities. What other processes need to be improved to free-up staff time to work on those priorities?
- Do you have a Lean coordinator and trained Lean facilitators? If you don't have an agency Lean coordinator, identify motivated change agents to head up the effort, and send them to Lean training.
- Are managers and rank-and-file employees aware of Lean and the expectations for their participation? If not, prepare a message announcing the Lean initiative and set the expectation that all employees will take the White Belt training.
- Convey your priorities to your agency's Lean coordinator and to your management team. Ask the Lean coordinator to work with managers to schedule projects for the priority areas.
- Expect the Lean coordinator to work with sponsors to prepare charters and schedule events, track the implementation, and report to the management team. Your coordinator should also network with other Lean practitioners to identify best practices, exchange facilitation resources, communicate about successes and build Lean culture.

SUMMARY OF LESSONS LEARNED

- Leaders at the top of the organization must show authentic commitment to the value of process improvement as a core component of their mission to serve their customers.
- While the Lean coordinator plays a very important part, the leader's role is fundamental to the success of the initiative; the other roles

emanate from that. As noted in a GFOA White Paper, "A coordinator is not a substitute for consistent and conspicuous support from the organization's leadership, or for the engagement of the Lean event sponsor or the Lean team leader in both the Lean event and follow-up activities."[14]

The optimal working model has a role for everyone in the organization:

- Top management articulates strategic priorities and key performance indicators (KPIs): the foundation of Lean project charters.
- Lean coordinators work with management to track the progress and report the metrics. The Lean coordinator or a member of the agency Lean team works with the sponsor to construct the draft charter, schedule the event and identify a facilitator.
- Division directors and bureau chiefs sponsor the *kaizen* events, approve the changes, and assure implementation. If a project requires personnel from multiple bureaus, the sponsor should be someone with authority over those bureaus. The Lean coordinator or a member of the agency Lean team constructs the draft charter, schedules the event, and identifies a facilitator.
- *Kaizen* teams document current workflow, identify improvements, design the future work flow, with task/timeline implementation plan, and present it to the sponsor. Each team needs a project manager who will track the progress of the implementation plan and update all team members and the sponsor. If necessary, the sponsor seeks assistance from upper management, as appropriate, to assure follow through on implementation.
- Everyone celebrates the wins and builds Lean culture.

APPLYING THE LESSONS

- The chief executive officer articulates unambiguous support for the initiative and requires each department head to schedule a Lean for Leaders workshop for their management teams.
- The Lean for Leaders workshop is offered in the Certified Public Manager (CPM) program.

- The commissioner of each agency appoints a Lean coordinator and sets the expectation that everyone in the agency will participate.
- Equal access to training is available, regardless of funding source. Supervisors assist by modifying schedules and plans for coverage, so staff can attend training.

NOTES

1 Katherine Barrett and Richard Greene, *Grading the States: A Management Report Card* (p. 32), Pew Charitable Trusts, Governing Magazine (March 2008).

2 "Report of the Governor's Commission on Innovation, Efficiency, and Transparency," Submitted to Governor Maggie Hassan on January 19, 2015 (50). Accessed February 13, 2018. www.innovations.harvard.edu/sites/default/files/opex/documents/Report%20of%20the%20Governor%27s%20Commission%20on%20Innovation%2C%20Efficiency%2C%20and%20Transparency%2C%20New%20Hampshire%2C%202015.pdf.

3 John Bicheno and Matthias Holweg, *The Lean Toolbox 5th Edition* (Picsie Books, 2016), 90.

4 Jim Womack, *Gemba Walks* (The Lean Enterprise Institute, Cambridge, 2011) 92.

5 The Shingo Institute, "The Shingo Model for Operational Excellence," p. 11.

6 Shayne Kavanagh and David Krings, "The Eight Sources of Waste and How to Eliminate Them," *Government Finance Review*, December 2011, 19.

7 "Dr. Deming's 14 Points for Management," The Deming Institute. Accessed February 13, 2018. https://deming.org/explore/fourteen-points.

8 Jim Womack, *Gemba Walks* (The Lean Enterprise Institute, Cambridge, 2011) 68.

9 Jim Lancaster, *The Work of Management: A Daily Path to Sustainable Improvement* (The Lean Enterprise Institute, Cambridge, 2017).

10 Mike Rother, *Toyota Kata* (McGraw-Hill Education, 2010) 15.

11 The Shingo Institute, "The Shingo Model for Operational Excellence", p. 3.

12 The Shingo Institute. Accessed February 27, 2018. https://shingo.org/.

13 Jim Womack, *Gemba Walks* (The Lean Enterprise Institute, Cambridge, 2011) 70.

14 Shayne Kavanagh, "Less Time, Lower Cost, and Greater Quality: Making Government Work Better with Lean Process Improvement," White Paper, Government Finance Officers Association (25).

8

Run Government Like a Business

Larry started every campaign speech the same way. "We need to run government a business—my business experience makes me the right choice to represent this district." Well-respected in the community for operating the local market in the center of town, Larry easily won a term in the state legislature.

When he took office, Larry voted against budget proposals for a range of government expenditures. He led the fight to slash line items for equipment purchases, facilities maintenance, and staff training. He supported the continuation of a yearlong hiring freeze.

Yet, these policies did not yield the expected results. Larry's constituents began calling him to complain about long waits for routine items such as license renewals or building permits. They wanted him to fix it.

Falling asleep that night, asking himself what else could be done to run government like a business, Larry woke up at his market. A series of odd events took place ...

Sally, the longtime manager of the market, announced that she was retiring and moving out of the state, but she had a great candidate in mind to step into the position. Larry and Sally interviewed the candidate and offered him the job on the spot, which he accepted immediately. Suddenly, a deep, booming voice announced "NO! You can't violate the hiring freeze!" Larry was startled. He replied, "Please—this is a critical position for my business—can't you make an exception?" The voice answered: "Some limited exceptions are permitted." "Certainly, this would qualify for an exception," Larry pleaded. "I can't run my business without a manager." The voice replied, "Perhaps. The committee meets on the 15th of each month. To get on the agenda, you must complete a justification request documenting the impact and submit it with the required signatures." "But we're entering the fall foliage tourist season," Larry protested. "We expect three tour buses to stop in our town each weekend—what if the committee won't give the approval to hire my manager?" "You can appeal, and have it reconsidered in a subsequent meeting," replied the voice.

Larry struggled through the start of the tourist season without a manager. Without a replacement for Sally, the stock was not efficiently managed—they ran out of popular items and had a surplus of others. Perishable overstock went to waste. Larry tried to keep track of employees' schedules, but he ended up filling in when unexpected absences occurred. He was exhausted, yet he could see that his customer service continued to decline in quality, along with his profit margin.

Then, with a busload of tourists about to arrive, one of the three cash registers broke down. Larry called the company and asked for an emergency repair call and rush order replacement. He had done business with this company for years, and the manager immediately agreed to accommodate Larry's schedule.

The voice boomed, "NO! You cannot violate the contracting and purchasing policy!" "What?" Larry cried. "I've done business with this company for years! They always treat me fairly." "Every 2 years, you must put your equipment maintenance contract out to bid," explained the Voice. "Okay—maybe I can't do the maintenance now—but can I please buy a new cash register?" Larry begged. "I'm sorry," responded the voice. "There is a freeze on equipment purchases."

The wait for service in Larry's market grew longer as customers lined up to check out at the two remaining registers. Lines backed up into the aisles, blocking access to products. Some customers left in frustration.

Then, an early-season storm arrived, blanketing the parking lot in three feet of snow. Larry called the company that provided snow removal service and scheduled a time to clear the lot.

The voice returned: "NO! The facilities maintenance budget has been eliminated for the remainder of the calendar year. The committee did not anticipate significant snowfall prior to January." Larry did not bother asking if he could appeal the committee's decision. He took his old snow blower out of the storage shed and it took him all morning to clear the parking lot. By that time, his early-bird customers had gone to another store.

The next day, Larry jumped out of bed with a new mission: "Let's run government like a Lean business!"

He led the charge to repeal the hiring freeze and restore the funding for equipment and facilities maintenance. He persuaded his colleagues to disband the committees that micromanaged hiring and purchasing, allowing public managers to move budgetary line items based on business needs.

Larry introduced legislation allowing agencies to roll over 20% of unexpended funds to the following year and tasking agency heads with long-term planning for equipment replacement and facilities maintenance. He recruited a team of the state's leading technology experts to examine the archaic IT systems and make recommendations for appropriate upgrades to be considered in the next budget cycle.

Most importantly, he persuaded the governor to issue an executive order requiring all agencies to use Lean management and process improvement techniques. Agency heads were tasked with setting strategic goals according to the programmatic priorities established by the policy makers. The governor hired an experienced Lean practitioner to head a special Office of Operational Excellence. The initiative included basic Lean training for all state employees, the development of Lean practitioners, tracking the progress of the process improvements, and measuring the accomplishment of strategic goals.

Political question: Can a Lean management system flourish in a state with a political culture favoring a combination of budget cuts with layers of control? Would Larry lose the next election because he voted to fund the Office of Operational Excellence, or would he educate his constituents on the value of Lean management?

As noted in a White Paper published by the Government Finance Officers Association, "Public managers are often asked to 'trim the fat' in times of revenue scarcity. Unfortunately, there is no line item in the budget called 'fat.'"[1]

In the blog *Public Great*, Ken Miller refers to "the same old playbook—hiring freezes, travel restrictions, delaying maintenance," resulting in "tired, overworked employees trying to do the same operations with fewer resources." *The Lean Handbook* considers the long-term impact of misplaced efforts, noting, "Since many cost-cutting initiatives reduce expenses that do not appear to add immediate value (e.g. training, maintenance activities...), the impact of the reductions is eventually offset by increases in quality problems, lack of resources, and equipment problems."[2] Miller summarized that such approaches "create an illusion of efficiency. Real efficiency is about looking at the systems."[3]

SYSTEMS AND STRATEGY

Lean tools must be linked to organizational strategy. If Lean is only used to do projects, once the most painful processes have been improved, interest will wane. As a GFOA White Paper notes, "While Lean is powerful for making significant improvements in business process performance, it is a tactical tool. If it is not linked to broader organizational strategy, Lean can lose relevance to the organization members and be discontinued...Lean works best when it is treated as a discipline that is instilled into the fundamental way in which the organization thinks about service provision, rather than being treated as a one-off project. As such, public managers should carefully study Lean and consider how it might contribute to wider organization strategic objectives."[4]

As explained in the *McKinsey Quarterly*, "Initially, Lean was best known in the West by its tools: for example, *kaizen* workshops, where frontline workers solve knotty problems... In more recent years, this early (and often superficial) understanding of Lean has evolved into a richer appreciation of the power of its underlying management disciplines: putting customers first by truly understanding what they need and then delivering it efficiently; enabling workers to contribute to their fullest potential; constantly searching for better ways of working; and giving meaning to work by connecting a company's strategy and goals in a clear, coherent way across the organization."[5]

Throwing out the old playbook and adopting Lean management is not an easy path. Even if the state's governor understands and embraces the principles, he/she may not have the support of the legislature to appropriate necessary resources. Many states struggle to meet basic obligations. Employees, supervisors and managers alike experience the pressure of nearly constant *muri*. The best they can hope for is to keep up with the firefighting. Yet, Lean activists see signs of hope. While no model is perfect, there is much to be learned from those who have made progress on the journey.

Moving from the traditional "last year plus" incremental budget to a programmatic-based model is much more congruent with Lean management. The typical process of "last year plus" (or minus) does not correspond to reality. Lots of *muda* is built into that structure. If managers don't spend their entire budgets during the fiscal year, the elected officials are likely to give them less the following year, regardless of equipment or programmatic needs.

Recall our public-sector parable when Larry found himself in a dilemma because a machine he needed to replace immediately had to wait until the next budget cycle. Lean organizations only use the resources they need, and their leaders are empowered to allocate those resources. Necessary personnel can be hired, and equipment can be maintained. With the appropriate Lean training and the authority to manage his budget, Larry could manage a Lean operation. How would elected officials know that Larry was doing a good job? Measure the outcomes.

MEASUREMENTS THAT MATTER

How do we know that our Lean projects are improving meaningful outcomes in our states? Just because it's measurable doesn't make it meaningful. Sam McKeeman cautioned against measuring too much, or measuring the wrong things, or "gaming" the measurements to tell a favorable story.

It's tempting to tout the savings from process redesign by aggregating the shrinkage of cycle time, compared with work time. For example, the cycle time for the out-of-state travel permission process could be leaned from 225 hours to 1 hour; while the work time to complete the form might go from 80 minutes to 40 minutes.

The dramatically improved cycle time will certainly be good for morale, but the six weeks of process time was mostly the *muda* of waiting, not tied to any employee activity. The prompt booking of airfare, hotel reservations, and conference registration fees would avoid price increases common in the six-week process. Those dollars could be quantified as savings, or cost avoidance.

If the managers were removed from the signature chain, the work time saved per traveler per year could be aggregated. How would the time of the managers formerly on the signature chain be redeployed, and what could be accomplished if they focused on other matters?

FREED CAPACITY TO REDEPLOYED CAPACITY

Consider the example of a team of four people meeting for 2 hours. 2 hours multiplied by 4 equals 8 staff hours. If that meeting was cancelled, 8 hours of work could be redeployed. How can we quantify the value of those people spending their time differently?

In *The Kaizen Event Planner*, Karen Martin and Mike Osterling explain, "Freed capacity in the form of reduced process time should be used to absorb additional growth, perform more value-added work, reduce overtime, and support continuous improvement activities."[6]

Dr. Darlene Dumont of the Lean Enterprise Institute notes that redeployed time can be quantified by calculating the improvement in the ratio of value added to non-valued added time as a percentage of the overall process. Using the metrics from your data sheets, it is possible to calculate the non-value-added (NVA) ratio as a percentage and show the improvement as a reduction in your NVA% or an increase in your value-added (VA) time. The comparison between the current state and future state can document the organization's ability to generate more value for effort. In health care, for example, less time on *muda* means that more time can be devoted to patient care.

Measurement systems are central to the results-based approach being implemented by progressive leaders in several states. According to the case study, "Performance Management and Lean Process Improvement," the State of Washington saved "one million hours of time saved waiting in Department of Licensing lobbies using process improvements and partnering with private driver-training schools."[7]

Improved processes that require fewer labor-hours allow staff to catch up on backlogs and keep current with the work. Staff can be redeployed to mission critical tasks, appropriately aligning skill sets.

One such example can be found in New Hampshire, with the use of civilian employees for tasks that do not require powers of arrest to replace state troopers for certain duties. New Hampshire's Innovation Commission reported that civilian mechanics had been assigned to conduct compliance visits to auto dealers and inspection stations, and that DOS was "replacing troopers with civilians under supervision of a trooper to conduct commercial vehicle (CDL) license exams and road tests. These civilian employees will also be extensively used in the annual inspection of all school buses in the state."[8]

When quantifying the gains from this event, it's important to avoid the temptation to tally the cost of the troopers' salaries and benefits for the hours formerly spent on those tasks, and claim it as savings. The troopers were not laid off; they were redeployed to job duties more appropriate to their specialized training and skill sets. The challenge is determining a meaningful measurement for the public benefit from having more troopers on the road, and the increased safety inspections by the civilian employees.

Appropriate outcome indicators can be used to evaluate a correlation between the redeployed capacity and a quality improvement. For example, tracking the annual number of highway accidents could identify a potential correlation between the resources allocated for highway safety and the accidents. New Hampshire's DOS is working to develop meaningful metrics for the department's primary activities. The agency is using software capable of graphically tracking the trends, which can provide data indicating correlations between resources and outcomes.

As organizations seek to correlate inputs to outcomes, the identification of meaningful measurements comes first—also known as the "so-what?" factor.

Suppose we trained hundreds of employees in Lean White Belt, but never conducted any *kaizen* events? Should we measure the percentage of employees trained in the workforce, compared with the number of *kaizens*? Those are outputs. It would be more meaningful to compare the percentage of employees who are trained in Lean and track a potential correlation to the outcomes: the savings of time for routine processes, increased customer satisfaction and the achievement of organizational priorities.

It requires expertise to develop appropriate metrics that can distinguish causality from correlation, filtering what researchers consider "noisy data" prior to establishing links between inputs and outcomes. After deciding what to measure, data need to be collected and analyzed.

In *Government That Works*, John M. Bernard describes the efforts of states that have successfully linked process improvement to measurable gains in outcomes. Bernard prescribes the use of "results-driven management" using meaningful metrics. Among other examples, Bernard cited data gathered in Colorado that linked specific policy initiatives to a 40% reduction in unintended teen pregnancies, and Maryland's quantifiable efforts to increase transit ridership and renewable energy use.

Can these lessons apply to Lean initiatives? According to Bernard's book and a case study published by Harvard's Kennedy School of Government, the State of Washington has linked process improvement initiatives with meaningful measurements of public policy goals.

WASHINGTON

The state of Washington is a story of starting from the top and going up. Although no state received an A grade in 2008, Washington was one of three states that earned an A-minus. The Pew report noted: "Washington has been a consistent leader in results-based governance. It was ahead of nearly all other states in controlling spending by keeping track of where investments were and were not paying off." The Pew report also praised Governor Christine Gregoire's Government Management Accountability and Performance program (GMAP). The state's commitment to excellent public service continued under Gregoire's successor, Jay Inslee. The "Results Washington" initiative is an exemplar among state Lean programs, documented in *Government That Works* and the focus of a case study published by the Kennedy School of Government. Rather than calling it "Lean management," the case study breaks it into two components—"performance management and employee-driven process improvement."[9]

Results Washington is within the office of the governor and is tasked with developing strategic improvement plans to manage, monitor, and implement the five priority goals of this initiative: (1) World-Class Education; (2) Prosperous Economy; (3) Sustainable Energy and a Clean Environment; (4) Healthy and Safe Communities; and (5) Effective, Efficient, and Accountable Government.[10]

RHODE ISLAND

In 2015, Rhode Island Governor Gina Raimondo issued an executive order requiring the use of Lean throughout state government. The state that received the grade of C-minus in the 2008 Pew report (just above NH's D-plus) has progressively moved forward with Lean. Below is an excerpt from the executive order:

"Whereas, the citizens of Rhode Island deserve a government that provides services effectively and efficiently; and Whereas, cultivating a culture of continuous improvement in State government will make State programs and processes more customer-service oriented...Whereas, empowering State employees to step back from their daily work and apply Lean methodology to review existing processes will lead to focusing on and improving the work…Therefore…All executive branch departments and agencies in the Governor's Cabinet shall integrate Lean process improvement efforts…"[11]

The EO included specific requirements, including deadlines for departments with the most public-facing functions to complete initial Lean training and at least two process improvement reviews. Agencies were required to report annually to the Office of Management & Budget OMB) and the Governor's Office, including summaries of completed and pending Lean process reviews, number of trainings held, and measurable outcomes. The initiative has a statewide Lean coordinator within OMB's Office of Performance Management. Leadership and expertise have been developed so that each agency has a Lean Ambassador trained to coordinate projects. Since 2015 more than 2,800 state employees have received Lean 101 training and state agencies have conducted more than 100 projects.[12]

NEW HAMPSHIRE

Our New Hampshire Lean initiative has received support from three governors:

> Since I became governor, I have focused on finding ways to make government work better for the citizens of New Hampshire. By seeking to continuously improve the way we do business, we are able to offer better service to New Hampshire citizens—our customers—and to make better use of scarce resources. I applaud the use of Lean and other techniques that have allowed state agencies to streamline processes, improve response times, and provide better service to the citizens and businesses of our state.

> *John H. Lynch, Governor of New Hampshire, 1/6/2005-1/3/2013*

> Encouraging innovation in how the State of New Hampshire provides essential public services is a critical aspect of maintaining fiscal responsibility and protecting taxpayer dollars. I strongly support the continued use of Lean process improvement tools as a proven means to ensure that public funds are used as efficiently and effectively as possible. We owe the citizens of the Granite State a government that is committed to eliminating waste. By focusing on collective problem-solving in order to deliver services as efficiently as possible, Lean is helping us build a stronger, more innovative New Hampshire.

> *Maggie Hassan, Governor of New Hampshire, 1/3/2013-1/2/2017*

Governor Christopher Sununu, who succeeded Governor Hassan, signed the charter of our Lean Executive Committee, with our mission: "To promote a stronger, more efficient New Hampshire, the Lean Executive Committee provides education, innovation, advocacy and facilitation of Lean process improvement." The document closed with: "The New Hampshire Governor, Christopher T. Sununu, endorses the work of the Lean Executive Committee and is committed to the training models, work of Lean Practitioners, and Lean as a tool for process improvement across State Government." It was signed on July 26, 2017.[13]

During each of these three administrations, we had hopes for the establishment of a state-level Office of Lean to coordinate the initiative. We were discouraged when the New Hampshire legislature declined to establish an office of process improvement, or innovation initiatives proposed by Governor Lynch and by Governor Hassan. Finally, under Governor Sununu, the legislature approved two positions for a Project Management, Innovation, and Operational Analysis unit within the Department of Administrative Services. However, the unit was tasked with implementing IT projects, linking over 40 agencies into a common timekeeping and payroll system. Firefighting took priority, removing the word "innovation" from the unit's title. The long-awaited central Lean office would have to wait.

As of 2018, all but three of New Hampshire's agency Lean coordinators were doing their Lean work as a sideline to their primary job duties, and no one had the responsibility or authority to organize cross-agency initiatives. We came close in 2018—it was a near miss. We couldn't get coordination at the strategic level.

VERMONT

While New Hampshire's "night shift" struggled to gain ground, across the river in Vermont, a different model was emerging. On his first day in office, January 5, 2017, Governor Phil Scott issued two related executive orders establishing the Program to Improve Vermont Outcomes Together (PIVOT)[14] and the Government Modernization & Efficiency Team (GMET). Both PIVOT and GMET are intended "to empower state employees with modernized IT systems and training, and implement a customer-focused culture across state government." The governor stated,

"These executive orders lay the groundwork for our efforts to make state government more effective for the people of Vermont. Every day, we will be guided by our strategic goals, working to create more economic opportunity, help working families keep more of what they earn, and protect our most vulnerable. If everyone in state government pulls in the same direction—towards these goals—we will move Vermont forward to a more prosperous future."[15]

The PIVOT EO sought to leverage and expand specific ongoing continuous improvement efforts occurring at the Department of Environmental Conservation (DEC), Agency of Transportation (AOT), and Agency of Human Services (AHS). Both DEC and AOT had been running successful Lean programs for a few years, and AHS had been utilizing Result-Based Accountability (RBA) in addition to an approach called AIM based on the PDCA cycle.

Like many executive orders, several tasks and associated deadlines were established. In addition to mandatory executive branch appointing authority training and the development of a program inventory, secretaries and commissioners were instructed to identify continuous improvement leads and teams to help coordinate continuous improvement activities within each agency and independent department. Like other states, a PIVOT Steering Committee was created comprised of these leads. They work with the CPO to identify opportunities for cross-agency collaboration and resource sharing. This structure facilitates the prioritization of strategic improvement events that impact business processes in a shared service delivery system. The committee ensures the consistent and effective use of Lean, RBA, and other continuous improvement techniques.

What was not listed in the PIVOT EO were the specifics of exactly how PIVOT would function and lead to better results for Vermonters. As we know, programs are made up of much more than just edicts and deadlines. To help build the program and define its major elements, Governor Scott tapped seasoned Lean coordinators from AOT and DEC as well as the Director of Performance Improvement at AHS. For roughly the first year, Paul Keegan (AOT), Justin Kenney (DEC), and Dru Roessle (AHS) were assigned to work 60% of their time with the State's Chief Performance Officer (CPO), Sue Zeller.

During this time, they started to put together the pieces of a groundbreaking initiative that attempted to fully merge the world of RBA and Lean under the umbrella of continuous improvement. Through a robust training program, staff at all levels are taught not only to solve problems using a variety of tools, but to see problems in a larger context by utilizing ends to means thinking. In this way, PIVOT bakes in what most Lean initiatives lack: the "so what" factor. It aims to move the state from random to strategic acts of improvement. Most practitioners know that Lean can be used to increase customer value and improve efficiency—but, how can it be used to meet the strategic goals of growing the economy, making Vermont more affordable, and protecting the vulnerable? Essentially, PIVOT is intended "to create a continuous improvement culture and system which integrates top down vision with bottom up ideas."[16]

There are many more aspects in the PIVOT initiative that are beyond the scope of this overview. The big news is that next phase of Lean innovation is alive and well in Vermont. The potential of RBA-linked Lean initiatives is an incredible breakthrough in public management.

Consider the contrast with New Hampshire's Lean Executive Committee, which has neither a connection to the state's strategic goals, nor the authority to organize cross-agency projects. We've been able to organize a few cross-agency projects, anyway. More about that later.

MUDA IN GOVERNMENT PROCUREMENT

Before leaving the topic of results-driven management, let's take a quick look at a topic that can't easily be addressed, but is worth noting. The well-intended policies established to fight corruption result in significant *muda*. Sam McKeeman noted that government procurement is the antithesis of Lean; he explained that the U.S. military used to be able to build a battleship in days; current procurement methods disperse construction of military aircraft among defense contractors in dozens of states. As Lean practitioners know, increasing the number of hand-offs increases the cycle time, the cost, and the likelihood of defects.

Sam explained that Toyota brings in several potential suppliers, describes the product requirements, and discusses price and quality. Once a supplier is selected, the company will continue to do business with them, unless there is a reason to discontinue.

Consider Deming's Point #4: "End the practice of awarding business on the basis of price tag. Instead, minimize total cost. Move toward a single supplier for any one item on a long-term relationship of loyalty and trust."[17]

In New Hampshire, sole-source contracting is frowned upon by the Executive Council as a non-competitive practice, and all contracts are required to be approved by this elected body of five executive councilors. The result is a constant contracting process for most contracts being bid out every 2 years. The bidding and procurement process takes an average of 9 months. You don't have to pass advanced calculus to see how this math works against the wind of Lean efficiency. To make matters worse, a commissioner of one of the largest agencies recently decided to read every RFP, bottlenecking another level of review. The *muda* in New Hampshire's system of control will be discussed in more detail in later in this chapter.

Developing countermeasures to reduce *muda* in procurement processes would be different for each level of government. If one were to apply the 5 Whys to the dispersion of defense contracts among states, it's possible that one of the root causes would be identified as members of Congress using defense spending as a multi-state jobs program. Developing countermeasures for that cause would likely prove challenging, but other causes might be identified and addressed.

The *muda* in the typical low-bid requirements could be identified, but perhaps not easily removed. Public managers are not obligated to accept bids that don't meet the specifications, but it is difficult to prepare specs that anticipate every contingency. Developing a request for proposal (RFP) can take months, particularly if the proposal requires IT expertise. Once a vendor is selected, it is equally challenging to manage the deliverables.

It would be interesting to convene a Lean event to review the steps in a procurement process. Consider the following problem statement: "How can the government procure timely, cost-effective, quality products?" The team could evaluate the steps that are value-added, non-value-added (*muda*), and non-value-added but necessary to the institution. Who would be the best sponsor for such a project, and who would be needed on the team?

NON-STANDARD ADOPTION OF STANDARD BUSINESS PRACTICES

Customers of private-sector goods and services are accustomed to conducting business online, and these conveniences are steadily being adopted in the public sector. The path to implementation, however, is far from smooth. Below is an example of the use of an A3 format to address non-standard acceptance of e-signatures. The A3 is followed by a work-sheet using the 5 Whys to dig deeper into the reasons for managers' hesitation to authorize the acceptance of e-signatures.

Background

Business case: Based on a customer satisfaction survey, the option to use e-signatures is increasingly important to our agency's customers. It also frees up time for staff to redeploy their efforts to strategic priorities

Current Conditions

Several divisions within the agency are using e-signatures, while others are not

Problem statement: How can we provide the e-signature option for all agency customers?

Goals and Targets

Implement the e-signature option for 50% of the agency's programs within 90 days, 75% within 120 days, and 100% within a year

Root Cause Analysis

- E-signature set up requires IT assistance and not all divisions have access to IT resources
- Some programs have a wet-signature requirement in statute or rule. Why? Statutes and rules are enacted over time, specific to each program, generally lacking in consistent standards and without regard to efficient operation
- Even if wet signatures are not required, some managers will not allow it (see 5 Whys below) ... The culture is risk-averse

Countermeasures

- To address the uneven availability of IT resources: authorize an agency-wide initiative so that the e-signature option is designed as a standard feature equally available in all units
- To address the units that are governed by statute or rule requiring wet signatures: request appropriate changes from policy makers
- To address risk-averse culture: assemble a team to conduct a risk assessment

Plan

- The commissioner issues a directive explaining that the use of a widely accepted business practice is good customer service, not an abuse of authority
- Employees track the amount of time spent on processing paper copies
- A team of unit managers and IT managers design the implementation to commence within 45 days in units where there is no wet signature requirement
- The agency's legislative liaison work with policy makers on any necessary changes to law and/or rule

Sustainment

- Project manager to track progress and send Gantt chart to team members every 30 days tracking project progress; contact sponsor to troubleshoot as needed
- Customer satisfaction surveys to elicit feedback as units come on board with the e-signature option
- Employees track the time savings and report on how the time is used to accomplish other priorities

5 WHYS

The abnormal condition	Some units within the agency will not accept electronic signatures, even if wet signatures are not required by the laws or rules pertaining to their unit
Why?	They are waiting for permission from the legal department
Why?	The legal department is considering whether managers must be granted explicit permission in law or rule
Why?	One manager asked the legal department if it was okay to accept electronic signatures, so the legal department started a review. Other managers heard that the legal department was reviewing the question, so they decided to wait for the answer
Why?	A risk-averse culture has developed
Why?	The department was sued once for over-reaching its authority under statute or rule, so it is now common practice to ask permission prior to making decisions

ASSESSING *MUDA* IN ORGANIZATIONAL CONTROL

Institutions, both public and private, need to balance customer convenience with organizational integrity. Customers' data must be secure; their appreciation of a prompt transaction would vanish if the price of expediency includes an increased risk for identity theft. Public organizations, particularly those entrusted with personal medical information, must be vigilant about IT security.

As stewards of the public funds, agencies must also guard against misappropriation and embezzlement. How many checks and balances are enough? How should we balance consideration of risk with the mission of customer service?

There is an interesting paradox in the actions of those who believe in limited government and who are distrustful of government. The multiple layers of checking thicken the bureaucracy and impede efficient operation. However, those who are suspicious are reluctant to cut this aspect of government, due to a belief that it creates accountability. Perhaps they don't see the paradoxical effect. The clearest example is in a layer of government that only exists in New Hampshire—the five-member executive council, which reapproves expenditures and fund transfers already budgeted and approved by legislative action.

> The New Hampshire Executive Council holds the distinction of being the first and the last of its kind in the nation. It is a vestige of the Colonial era and a public reminder of the continuing indication of the basic distrust Granite State citizens have for dictatorial government.[18]

The Council deals with matters as trivial as tuition reimbursement for individual employees. Movement of funds from one agency to another, and transfer of funds from the federal government to municipalities, is also routed through the Council. As the Pew report noted in 2008, "Much work gets held up until the council meets and approves expenditures ranging from $60 million for a new management information system to a $930 trip to Delaware for three Fish and Game officials."[19]

The *muda* is consequential. Documents required by the Council are prepared by employees working at the program level and administrative levels throughout state government. Following the internal agency review, the documents are reviewed by the Attorney General's office and the Department of Administrative Services (DAS). When Roberta and Chris leaned the preparation process internal to the Department of Safety in 2009, they saved time by avoiding rework when the agency's documents were rejected by DAS. Agencies that have not leaned their preparation process continue to deal with work and rework.

When Lean Black Belt John MacPhee worked to Lean the contracting process for DHHS (2010–2014), he presented the process map to the Council, so they could see the arduous process. Several Councilors were persuaded to raise the threshold requiring G&C review from $10,000 to $25,000. One of the Councilors, Colin Van Ostern, made the case in a guest editorial prior to the vote. He explained, "Today, a typical contract of less than $25,000 consumes roughly 40 to 85 hours of personnel time and costs the state nearly $3,000 (as estimated by the Division of Purchase & Property Management). There are hundreds of contracts of this size (last year, 374 to be precise). Quite literally, we have dozens of state employees who spend hundreds or thousands of hours a year on paperwork on these contracts. It's not uncommon for an agency to receive an electronic document from a vendor, print it out and ship it to another agency that makes a dozen or more paper copies for processing, then scans one into a new electronic document.[20]

Consider the staff effort that could be redeployed to other priorities, averaging the estimated 40–85 staff hours multiplied by the 374 contracts of amounts less than $25,000. $62.5 \times 374 = 23,375$ staff hours.

On September 17, 2014, the Council amended their procedures requiring agencies to submit contracts for approval, increasing the threshold from $10,000 to $25,000.

While this change reduced significant *muda*, other archaic oversight requirements persisted. According to the minutes of the March 21, 2018[21] meeting, in addition to authorizing an employee to take two courses at the local community college, the council authorized four employees in the Department of Agriculture to travel more than 300 miles in a state vehicle, and they authorized the Department of Environmental Services to make a $200,000 grant to the City of Portsmouth from the Drinking Water/Ground Water Trust Fund.

It would be instructive to prepare a fiscal impact statement to determine the cost of this layer of government. Yet there are those who believe that the expense is worthwhile due to a belief that this extra level of oversight deters waste or malfeasance.

A Lean manager would work with a team to develop appropriate countermeasures to prevent against fraud or theft, without crippling business or requiring thousands of hours of employees' time. The next section explores the possibility of a responsible middle ground.

RESPONSIBLE RISK MANAGEMENT

Impatient Lean activists are tempted to minimize concerns about risk, but responsible improvements must take risk into account. Public organizations need to figure out how best serve their customers while protecting organizational integrity and security.

In *Lean Processes without Compromising Controls*, the authors address the topic of how "controls can be designed into Lean processes without compromising the effectiveness of Lean initiatives." They refer to the Committee of Sponsoring Organizations of the Treadway Commission (COSO) for guidance on "the right balance of efficiency, effectiveness, and minimal enterprise risk."[22] Among the recommendations is to conduct a risk assessment of impact and likelihood using a grid format. The table below is based on the authors' model:

High likelihood of occurrence	High impact
Low likelihood of occurrence	Low impact

The authors conclude, "designing Lean business processes with control considerations does not mean 'putting up with fat.'" They recommend that Lean teams integrate the risk assessment (likelihood and impact) with "the decisions to apply a control and the choice of a control strategy."[23]

The following exercise about motivation for control mechanisms might generate some interesting discussion. What do you think are the primary reasons for layers of approval? Make a check mark next to the top three reasons:

- Due diligence
- The next level up (top management or political leaders) require a trail of accountability
- Fear of bad press
- Risk of embezzlement
- Risk of legal liability
- CYA
- Lack of trust in subordinates
- Concern about negative audit findings
- Past practice—that's the way it's always been done

SUMMARY OF LESSONS LEARNED

- The executive branch of state government seldom functions as a single organization; rather it is a series of subsystems. It siloed into agencies, with bureaus and subdivisions within each agency. Variation in statutory regulations diffuses responsibility and authority. Establishment of standard work across the enterprise is an elusive, but not impossible task, with the appropriate allocation of resources for a comprehensive Lean initiative.
- Running government like a business means a Lean business—where the focus is continuous improvement for the customer, and the management has the personnel and technology necessary for efficient operations.
- Elected officials and administrators add redundant layers of red tape to government operations believing that they are fostering accountability. Such policies do the opposite, diffusing responsibility and clogging operations.

- Lean managers seek to align authority and responsibility at the lowest possible level, assuring that everyone in the organization is well trained, competent, and committed to the mission.
- Practitioners should be aware of the work being done in the field of Lean risk assessment. The Government Finance Officers Association has published white papers. Articles can be found in the professional journals such as *Government Finance Review*. Lean techniques can incorporate the responsible integration of financial controls with legal liability concerns, as we proceed on the path to bureaucracy reduction.

APPLYING THE LESSONS

- Elected and administrative leaders need to articulate the goals and priorities. Determine clear objectives that support those goals. Identify quantifiable indicators and deliverables.

  The best way to prove the value of Lean is by measuring outcomes that move us toward the fulfillment of those goals. Are we doing better at what we're been asked to do?
- Professionals in finance and legal departments should have Lean training and join Lean project teams. Together, these teams can review the risks and benefits of archaic policies and develop Lean quality control.

NOTES

1 Shayne Kavanagh, "Less Time, Lower Cost, and Greater Quality: Making Government Work Better with Lean Process Improvement," White Paper, Government Finance Officers Association (1). www.gfoa.org/sites/default/files/GFOALeanWhitePaper.pdf.

2 Anthony Manos and Chad Vincent, Editors, *The Lean Handbook* (ASQ Quality Press, Milwaukee, WI, 2012) 288.

3 Ken Miller, "Lean Government's Promise of Going 'Lean'," Posted on *Public Great*, May 21, 2009. www.governing.com/blogs/public-great/lean-government.html.

4 Shayne Kavanagh, "Less Time, Lower Cost, and Greater Quality: Making Government Work Better with Lean Process Improvement," White Paper, Government Finance Officers Association (25–26). Accessed April 7, 2018. www.gfoa.org/sites/default/files/GFOALeanWhitePaper.pdf.

5 Ewan Duncan and Ron Ritter, "Next Frontiers for Lean," McKinsey Quarterly February 2014, McKinsey.com. Accessed April 21, 2018. www.mckinsey.com/insights/manufacturing/next_frontiers_for_lean.

6 Karen Martin and Mike Osterling, *The Kaizen Event Planner* (CRC Press, Taylor & Francis Group, LLC, Boca Raton, FL, 2007) 90.

7 Jane Wiseman, "Case Study: Performance Management and Lean Process Improvement—Results Washington, An Operational Excellence Government Success Story". Harvard Kennedy School, July 2017 (4). Accessed March 21, 2018. www.innovations.harvard.edu/opex/research/case-study-performance-management-and-lean-process-improvement-results-washington.

8 "Report of the Governor's Commission on Innovation, Efficiency, and Transparency," Submitted to Governor Maggie Hassan on January 19, 2015 (59). Accessed February 13, 2018. www.innovations.harvard.edu/sites/default/files/opex/documents/Report%20of%20the%20Governor%27s%20Commission%20on%20Innovation%2C%20Efficiency%2C%20and%20Transparency%2C%20New%20Hampshire%2C%202015.pdf.

9 Jane Wiseman, "Case Study: Performance Management and Lean Process Improvement—Results Washington, An Operational Excellence Government Success Story". Harvard Kennedy School, July 2017 (3). Accessed March 21, 2018. www.innovations.harvard.edu/opex/research/case-study-performance-management-and-lean-process-improvement-results-washington.

10 Jay Inslee, Governor of Washington, Executive Order 1304, Results Washington, Issued September 10, 2013. Accessed March 21, 2018. www.governor.wa.gov/sites/default/files/exe_order/eo_13-04.pdf.

11 Gina M. Raimondo, Governor of Rhode Island, "Lean Government Initiative" April 9, 2015. Accessed April 20, 2018. www.governor.ri.gov/documents/orders/ExecOrder_15-09_04092015.pdf.

12 Office of Performance Management—Lean RI. Aaccessed August 8, 2018. www.omb.ri.gov/performance/index.php#section3.

13 Lean Executive Committee Charter. Posted on the Lean.nh.gov website. Accessed April 15, 2018. http://lean.nh.gov/Documents/LEC%20Charter%202017.pdf.

14 Philip Scott, Governor of Vermont, PIVOT E.O. 17-04. Accessed April 18, 2018. http://governor.vermont.gov/sites/scott/files/documents/EO4PIVOT%20EO%20Final.pdf.

15 Office of Governor Phil Scott, "Governor Phil Scott Signs Four Executive Orders on First Day in Office," January 9, 2017. Accessed April 24, 2018. http://governor.vermont.gov/press-release/governor-phil-scott-signs-four-executive-orders-first-day-office.

16 Accessed April 24, 2018. http://spotlight.vermont.gov/performance-management.

17 "Dr. Deming's 14 Points for Management," The Deming Institute. Accessed February 13, 2018. https://deming.org/explore/fourteen-points.

18 "History of the New Hampshire Executive Council." Accessed April 15, 2018. www.nh.gov/council/history/index.htm.

19 Katherine Barrett and Richard Greene, *Grading the States: A Management Report Card* (p. 70), Pew Charitable Trusts, Governing Magazine (March 2008).

20 Colin Van Ostern, Executive Councilor, "Executive Council contract threshold should be raised," My Turn column published in the Concord Monitor on August 3, 2014. Accessed April 12, 2018. www.concordmonitor.com/home/12979481-95/my-turn-executive-council-contract-threshold-should-be-raised.

21 State of New Hampshire Executive Council website. "Meeting Minutes". Accessed April 7, 2018. http://sos.nh.gov/GC2.aspx.
22 Robyn L. Raschke, Michael T. Lee, and Arti Mann, "Lean Processes without Compromising Controls," *Government Finance Review*, 2013, *29*(3): 44–50. (45).
23 Robyn L. Raschke, Michael T. Lee, and Arti Mann, "Lean Processes without Compromising Controls," *Government Finance Review*, 2013, *29*(3), 44–50. (49–50).

9

Orange is the New Green

During the Yellow Belt classes, our *kaizen* teams are asked to identify the value of each step in the current state process. This chapter first revisits the core Lean concept of value for the customer, and the impact of the project teams. After considering the team dynamics, I'll propose an additional category to use in public sector processes responsible for enforcing regulations. We will explore the distinction between end-user customers and stakeholders, and how public employees have a responsibility to create value for both. First, a quick review of the basic red-green-yellow codes (Table 9.1).

YELLOW OR RED?

Yellow is non-value-added to the customer, but necessary for the operation of the institution. Examples include issuing payroll, maintaining an appropriate amount of record keeping, writing grants and reporting to funders. All activities that don't directly benefit the customer but are necessary for the continuation of the organization should be coded as yellow.

Not all Lean practitioners agree on the red vs. yellow distinction regarding policy requirements. Some practitioners consider all organizational policies as "business necessary" because they are required in the current process. I recommend that teams evaluate each requirement to distinguish business necessary requirements from *muda*. They will probably need to do some research. The 5 Whys root cause tool can assist them in evaluating the purpose of each requirement. Perhaps an extra layer of review was added because someone made a mistake once. If the regulation doesn't exist for a good reason, it should be coded as red. The team learns

TABLE 9.1

Categories and Color Codes for Value Assessment

Category	Color	Definition	Goal and Focus
Value Added	Green	• Transforms materials or information into products and services which the customer wants • The step adds a form or feature, moves it closer to final form, and the customer is willing to pay for the transformation	• Optimize to improve the efficiency and effectiveness of the task • Improve the flow • Monitor to meet customers' evolving requirements
Non-Value Added-Necessary	Yellow	• Essential to the overall business operations • Required by organization policy, law, or regulation for a valid reason (confirm by asking the 5 Whys)	• Verify that it is truly required • Redesign tasks to meet requirements more efficiently by mistake proofing the process
Non-Value Added	Red	• Consumes resources but does not directly contribute to the product or service • Required by organization policy, law, or regulation without a valid reason	• Eliminate • Work with the sponsor to eliminate non-value added, unnecessary regulations
Value-added to the public	Orange	Regulations that are valuable to the public, but not valued by the end-user customer	• Optimize to improve the efficiency and effectiveness of the task • Improve the flow

to identify *muda* as such, even if the sponsor lacks the power to eliminate unnecessary requirements.

While the team may struggle to differentiate yellow from red, it's an important conversation. Team members may become defensive, as portions of their work are labeled as *muda*—an understandable reaction. The facilitator should remind the team of the ground rule of "no blame." Reiterate that it is not a reflection of our personal value as employees if some of our work does not add value to the customer. We're doing this Lean project to improve customer value. To improve, we are evaluating the process, not ourselves. It can still be a touchy subject.

The Lean Toolbox addresses the issue, noting, "For example, many clerical procedures, one may argue that the customer is never happy to pay.

To call activities non-value added-necessary can be both unhelpful or demotivating to employees—how would you like to spend most of your time doing necessary non-value added work?"[1] The facilitator should remind the team that the overall process is valuable to the customer and everyone plays a part, and that the planned improvements will free up time for employees to do other valuable work.

Moving from the basic value assessment and color coding of green, yellow, and red, let's consider adding the category of orange to mean value-added to the public.

THE CASE FOR ADDING ORANGE

In adapting Lean for the public sector, it is useful to understand a dynamic tension in many governmental processes. The end-user customers are applicants for building permits, drivers' licenses, disability claims, and so on. Other customers are seeking to acquire copies of public records, borrow library books, or report an emergency. There are many of reasons to use the services of a government agency that most of us don't think about until we need the service.

While each of us is a customer when we use specific services as individuals, government also serves a broad purpose for the public at large. Governmental systems are in place so that people can expect safe buildings, bridges, food, pharmaceuticals, the judicious use of public funds, and so on. Members of the public rely on regulatory processes for these purposes. They are stakeholders in the system.

Ideally, both customers and stakeholders agree on the value of fair, transparent and efficient processes. Through this lens, both the end-user customer and the public are well served by Lean—because the focus is on quality as well as efficiency. Permit applicants, for example, appreciate the availability of courteous, professional staff to assist them in meeting the requirements. However, they may not appreciate the steps in the process that hold them accountable to meet health and safety codes.

Consider a Lean regulatory process. Permits are issued promptly to qualified customers; those who fail to qualify receive professional feedback as they endeavor to meet the requirements. Many of those customers would probably prefer to skip the permitting process, if they had the choice.

It's possible to educate permit applicants to appreciate the value of the regulations to the public. Teams should try to include these customers in their *kaizen* events, so permit applicants can learn about the reasons for the regulations. Working as a team, the customers and the employees can use the 5 Whys to consider the purpose of each regulation, as they evaluate the value of the steps in the process.

Once the applicants understand the value of regulations to protect the public, they might agree that the inspection is value-added. Arguably, though, those requirements still might not meet the definition of value from the customer's perspective. To the applicant, perhaps the only green in the permit application process is the step of issuing the permit. Yet the other steps have value to the public.

For example, the Department of Environmental Services (DES) issues administrative orders to cease activities that are polluting the environment. Improving the efficient dispatch of the order is unlikely to be valued by the person or business receiving that order. However, prompt enforcement of environmental standards benefits the public and mission of the agency. As Sam McKeeman noted, expeditious action can also deter other potential polluters. It's not about the number of orders issued; it's about the wetlands saved.

ASSESSING THE VALUE OF REGULATION

Lean teams that include administrative employees, end-user customers, and stakeholders will struggle with identification of value. In Lean manufacturing, value is added when a step transforms materials or information into products and services which the customer wants, and the customer is willing to pay for the transformation. In many governmental processes, there is more than one product: a specific deliverable such as a permit, and the public good. Consider two examples of regulatory processes:

Drivers' licenses: A post-9/11 regulation no longer allows licenses to be issued on the day of the application. Applicants are given a temporary paper copy, and the official license is subsequently mailed. The regulation's purpose was to confirm that people lived where they said they did, thereby making it more difficult to attain false documents. The regulation results in additional administrative costs and in a delay for applicants.

Determination of value by customers: Do applicants see the value of waiting to get their licenses?

Determination of value by the public: Do members of the public appreciate the purpose of this regulation?

Lean management perspective: Both the applicant and the public may agree that the regulation has value—but the level of their agreement may vary based on the amount of cost or inconvenience required to enforce it. A Lean event at the New Hampshire DMV improved the address confirmation process, reducing the cost of returned mail by $225,000. Prior to that Lean event, it was a much costlier regulation.

Food establishment licenses: A food safety inspection is required prior to granting a license to open restaurant.

Determination of value by the customers: Do restaurant owners see the value of the state or local health department confirming that their establishment is safe? Would they prefer receiving a license without an inspection?

Determination of value by the public: Do people think about health inspections when they eat at a restaurant? Do they assume that the food is safe because a regulatory process is in place?

Lean management perspective: Both the restaurant owner and the public may agree that the regulation has value. Responsible restaurant owners may appreciate a level playing field. If all operations are held to the same standard, they won't be undercut by those with shoddy operations. However, the level of their appreciation may vary based on the amount of cost or inconvenience required for enforcement, and the reasonableness of the inspection criteria. A Lean event can use the 5 Whys to evaluate the health and safety purposes for each of the food inspection standards. It can also identify the optimal administrative process and staffing level.

Building permits for multi-family residential construction: Developers are required to have a series of permits to build multi-family units.

Determination of value by the customer: Do developers see the value of the municipality confirming that their buildings are safe? Would they prefer receiving a permit without code inspections?

Determination of value by the public: Do people think about building permits and code inspections when renting an apartment? Do they assume that the building is safe because a regulatory process is in place?

Lean management perspective: Both the developer and the public may agree that the construction permitting process has value. Responsible developers will not be undercut by those using substandard materials. However, the level of their agreement with the process may vary based on the amount of cost or inconvenience required for enforcement, and the reasonableness of the inspection criteria. A Lean event can identify the safety purposes for the inspection standards, documenting its value. It can also consider the multiple types of permits typically required for a complex construction project and identify the optimal administrative process and staffing level.

Lean teams with administrative staff, end-user customers, and stakeholders may come to agreement about the value of each step in the process. However, it can be useful to differentiate the steps: which are value-added to the end-user customer—such as receiving the license or permit—compared with the steps that are value-added to the public—such as a code enforcement.

The differentiation between "green" and "orange" may not be necessary if the end-user customers and the stakeholders are both represented on the Lean team, and both see value in health and safety regulations. Drilling down, the team may identify portions of the regulatory standards that are obsolete. They might also identify archaic administrative regulations, such as requirements for notarized documents or original copies with wet signatures (Figure 9.1).

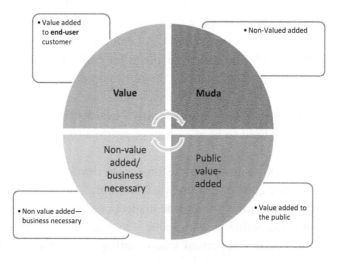

FIGURE 9.1
Four categories of value assessment.

ORANGE OR RED?

Not all regulations add value. Recall the discussion in Chapter 5 about the tendency of managers to make rules based on a single occurrence. Elected officials have the same inclination. The legislators who attended our early Lean training session understood that a common response to a constituent request is to introduce legislation. The adage "if the only tool you have is a hammer, everything looks like a nail" applies to elected officials. They're elected to be lawmakers, so they tend to make laws. The legislators in our session realized that it would be leaner to do research on the root cause of the problem and collaborate with colleagues for the best way to address it. While pride of authorship and the desire to claim political credit would work against such collaborative efforts, the concept is worth considering.

Existing laws and regulations can be examined as part of Lean projects. Ideally, lawmakers would join agency staff and customers on *Kaizen* teams to review processes, identify value to the public, and recommend ways to reduce *muda*. A useful trigger for these *kaizens* could be the performance audits conducted by the legislative budget assistance office (LBA). If every LBA audit triggered a *Kaizen* event, it could establish behaviors and set expectations that would create habits, building toward a culture of continuous improvement.

SUMMARY OF THE CASE FOR USING ORANGE

In the evolution of society, public safety via regulatory structures is integrated into the culture and through reasonable and practical laws, rules and policies. Orange is for civilization: value-added to the public. Regulations protecting consumers and the environment add the assurance that basic health and safety standards are being met.

De-bureaucratize: Use Lean tools to differentiate valuable regulations from *muda*. As with any Lean event, identify monuments and recommend removal of *muda*.

Optimize the value of regulation by designing processes with smooth flow and standard work. Lean teams recommend the use of checklists and website information to assist customers with online applications. *Kaizens* can make regulatory processes efficient, transparent, and customer-friendly.

EVALUATING PUBLIC GOOD

As *kaizen* teams consider the value of regulations, the criteria should be based on the regulation's purpose. The purpose may be obvious, such as regulations concerning the placement of smoke detectors in or adjacent to bedrooms. Others may be less apparent, such as a regulation requiring gifts to public agencies to be approved by the Executive Council, or for certain documents to be notarized. Teams can use the 5 Whys to examine the root cause of regulations with no apparent purpose. Once the purpose is determined, the team is better prepared to evaluate its public value.

Some process requirements are in place to foster public confidence, transparency and accountability. On balance, do the regulations add value, or just complexity and cost? Are there unintended negative consequences? Take the gift approval policy for example. Perhaps agencies should be able to accept donations of used office furniture or equipment without seeking permission from the Executive Council. If the team finds that the policy was created for transparency, perhaps there are other ways to make the gift known. Perhaps the Internet did not exist when the policy was established. Any alternative must be based on understanding why the policy exists.

Employees who work with these processes are in the best position to know if the rules and regulations are functioning as intended. This conversation needs to happen within the context of the organization's mission. Evaluate the purpose of the regulations and all organizational activities with respect to the purpose of the organization.

ORGANIZATIONAL MISSION

Both public and private sector organizations can be assessed based on purpose-driven activities. *The Lean Handbook* explains the distinction between companies that focus on making money compared with companies that focus on excellence.[2] Profits are a result, not a purpose. Mike Rother makes the same point in *Toyota Kata* where he quotes Alfred P. Sloan, the former president of General Motors: "We are not in the business of making cars, we are in the business of making money."[3] The contrast is evident when Rother notes Toyota's philosophy: "Survive long term as a company by improving and evolving how we make good products for the customer."[4]

There are numerous examples of private sector companies putting prof-its above the well being of their customers, employees, and the public at large. Human weaknesses such as carelessness or greed can result in mal-feasance or worse. The BP Deepwater Horizon explosion had devastat-ing consequences: 11 employees were killed, and millions of gallons of oil spewed into the Gulf of Mexico.

In the governmental sector, abuses and malfeasance can also take place. The lead poisoning of the population of Flint, Michigan, is one of the worst examples of public malfeasance.

These tragic consequences highlight the need for regulations. Protecting the public from wrong doing, by omission or commission. Checks and balances. Accountability.

While acknowledging the need for accountability, Lean practitioners seek to address the root causes of such problems, to reduce the likelihood of malfeasance. If the precursors can be dissected, proper countermea-sures can be developed.

Dr. Ginger Lever, Director of the New Hampshire Bureau of Education and Training, designed an ethics class with an exercise based on the Flint lead poisoning tragedy. The class is part of the core curriculum for the Certified Public Supervisor program. Using the event timeline based on source documents and media reports, the students create a flow chart of the decisions by elected officials, administrators, supervisors, employ-ees, Flint residents, and public health professionals. While reconstruct-ing the timeline, students evaluate the actions and motivations of officials at the state, local, and federal levels. How did this series of actions allow untreated river water to corrode the pipes and poison the city's water sup-ply? Which of the choices were incompetent, negligent, self-serving, or criminal? Where was the actor's decision-making lens focused—toward the community and customers and their interests, or inwardly for per-sonal interests? How did each decision contribute to the outcome and the type and level of response in the aftermath? The activity ends with a dis-cussion of the response that might be anticipated in New Hampshire.

Among the documents is one by an investigative reporter who found that "employees at the state's Department of Environmental Quality collected insufficient data and ignored the warning signs visible in what they did collect. In the process, they allowed the residents of Flint to be poisoned."[5]

This conduct was certainly contrary to the agency's articulated mission: "The Michigan Department of Environmental Quality (DEQ) promotes wise management of Michigan's air, land, and water resources to support a sustainable environment, healthy communities, and vibrant economy."[6]

There are multiple causes for the deviation from mission. For example, administrators may be tempted to betray public trust to curry favor with those in power. In *Leadership of Public Bureaucracies*, Larry D. Terry put a name to the self-serving careerism that compromises the integrity of the profession: administrative malpractice.[7] The malpractice can manifest itself in various ways. For example, a risk-averse bureaucrat may commit administrative malpractice through nonfeasance. While the failure to act is generally less apparent that overtly unethical acts, its impact is potentially devastating.

Lean managers realize the significance of everyone in the organization having a shared vision and purpose. According to *The Lean Handbook*, organizations that have a strong lean culture promote at least five cultural enablers (safety, standards, leadership, empowerment, and collaboration) … and they build their businesses on the core fundamentals of respect for individuals."[8]

The Shingo Institute's Model for Operational Excellence explains that "operational excellence requires a focus both on results and behaviors; and that ideal behaviors in an organization are those that flow from the principles that govern the desired outcomes…if it is to be sustained over the long-term; creating ideal, principle-based behaviors requires alignment of the management systems…[9]

The Shingo Model attests that "There is no greater measure of respect for the individual than creating a work environment that promotes both the health and safety of employees and the protection of the environment and the community. Environmental and safety systems embody a philosophical and cultural commitment that begins with leadership. When leadership is committed, then the organization creates and supports appropriate systems and behaviors."[10]

Strong organizational values must be articulated and modeled by top leadership and expected of all employees. Professional codes of conduct can also reinforce these guiding principles. Public administrators can refer to the Code of Ethics of the American Society for Public Administration (ASPA).[11] Among the Code's eight tenets are:

- Promote the interests of the public and put service to the public above service to oneself.

- Respect and support government constitutions and laws, while seeking to improve laws and policies to promote the public good.
- Be open, transparent, and responsive, and respect and assist all persons in their dealings with public organizations.

SUMMARY OF LESSONS LEARNED

- Governmental organizations have a dual responsibility: to our customers and to the public. The traditional Lean focus on value, as defined by the end-user customer, does not account for a divergence of interests in regulatory processes. Lean teams need to be aware that their customers and stakeholders may find value in different aspects of the process. Both customers and stakeholders must be respected in regulatory processes.
- Lean management is built on principle-driven behaviors as the foundation of operational excellence.

APPLYING THE LESSONS

- Governmental organizations can guard against malfeasance through rigorous fidelity to mission and unequivocal leadership. Provide ethics training that includes case studies, such as the Flint tragedy.
- Include customers, stakeholders, and policy makers in *kaizen* events. Use the 5 Whys to understand the purpose of regulations and legacy processes.
- When determining the value of each step in a regulatory process, consider adding the color code of orange to convey the value to the public.

NOTES

1 John Bicheno and Matthias Holweg, *The Lean Toolbox 5th Edition* (Picsie Books, 2016) 18.
2 Anthony Manos and Chad Vincent, Editors, *The Lean Handbook* (ASQ Quality Press, Milwaukee, WI, 2012) 287.

3 Mike Rother, *Toyota Kata* (McGraw-Hill Education, 2010) 62.

4 Mike Rother, *Toyota Kata* (McGraw-Hill Education, 2010) 38.

5 Anna Maria Barry-Jester, "What Went Wrong in Flint," Published on-line on FiveThirtyEight.com on January 26, 2016. Accessed June 5, 2018. https://fivethir-tyeight.com/features/what-went-wrong-in-flint-water-crisis-michigan/.

6 State of Michigan Departments. Accessed June 5, 2018. www.michigan.gov/som/0,4669,7-192-29701_29702_30045---,00.html.

7 Larry D. Terry, *Leadership of Public Bureaucracies: The Administrator as Conservator* (2nd ed.) (M.E. Sharpe, Inc., New York, 2003).

8 Anthony Manos and Chad Vincent, Editors, *The Lean Handbook* (ASQ Quality Press, Milwaukee, WI, 2012) 2.

9 The Shingo Institute. The Shingo Model for Operational Excellence (4).

10 The Shingo Institute. The Shingo Model for Operational Excellence (18).

11 American Society for Public Administration. Code of Ethics. Accessed June 3, 2018. www.aspanet.org/ASPA/Code-of-Ethics/ASPA/Code-of-Ethics/Code-of-Ethics.aspx?hkey=5b8f046b-dcbd-416d-87cd-0b8fcfacb5e7.

10

Paths through Muri

This chapter describes various components of strain and overburden. The most severe *muri* occurs when the organization lacks adequate staffing and resources to meet its core responsibilities. These conditions consume all the energy and creativity required to conduct a Lean initiative. A subtler but equally toxic *muri* results from of a lack of leadership for cultural transformation to a Lean management system. Before exploring potential countermeasures, let's review the impact of *muda* on our customers and *muri* on our employees:

As Lean moved from manufacturing to private sector service industries, practitioners continued to focus on the end-user customer who purchased the products and services. In government, our end-user customers are people seeking permits, licenses, or benefits, travelers on our roads and bridges, and so on. Both public and private sector organizations have customers—whether we are producing cars, bank statements, pizzas, permits, bridges, or birth certificates—we work in Lean teams to fight *muda* and maximize value for those customers.

Muri impedes our ability to fight *muda*. Consider the following analogy: Company owners and elected officials have similar roles in using their power to allocate resources in organizations. In the private sector, some owners sacrifice product quality and neglect customer service in pursuit of short-term profits. In the public sector, some elected officials seek political popularity by opposing adequate funding of public functions. These approaches both run contrary to principles of Lean management.

Lean can be sustainable in public sector organizations that provide the same components as successful initiatives in private industry: adequate staffing levels and the tools to accomplish the work. These circumstances are absent for many of us. In *Extreme Government Makeover*, Miller described the challenge: "Ravaged by years of budget cuts, reorganizations, and half-finished technology projects, the systems of government simply don't have the capacity to keep up.[1] A state bureau chief described the hollowed-out divisions as "a honeycomb of ineffective systems." *Muri* is formed by the pressure to keep up with the workload. *Muri* is compounded by the inability to accomplish our mission, which crushes morale and stomps out idealism.

In *The Lean Toolbox*, the authors suggested, "Perhaps *Muri* is the root problem. Overload causes stresses to people and may cause lack of maintenance for machines. This in turn causes variation—*mura*. Both then lead to *muda*. Frequently, as in value stream mapping, Lean begins with a *muda* hunt. Then, maybe *mura* is looked at and finally *muri*. A far better sequence is *muri, mura, muda*."[2]

COUNTERMEASURE TO *MURI*: RESPECT FOR PEOPLE

Principles identified by the Shingo Model for Operational Excellence offer guidance on avoiding *muri*. The model discusses the importance of leading with humility and respect, noting that "a leader's willingness to seek input, listen carefully, and continuously learn creates an environment where associates feel respected and energized and give freely of their creative abilities.

Alison Fisher, Program Director of LeanCT (State of Connecticut), explained, "Solving complex process, data, or policy problems is worthless without understanding the people behind it. The people we serve and the people who do the work are the most important aspects of all improvement activity. We typically discuss this as 'respect for people,' but it's so much more than that. One of the greatest lessons I've learned was from Ron Pereira at Gemba Academy. Ron told me that 'respect for people' in Japan isn't what we think it is here in the US. In Japan, it means understanding, seeing, and valuing a human being, their soul, and what they bring to an experience. It's not just speaking respectfully or pulling them into a meeting so they're not left out—it's honoring who they are and the benefit that they bring. In my mind, it's very similar to the Hindi phrase, *namaste*, which loosely translates to 'the light/divine in me recognizes the light/divine in you.'

Without the recognition of true respect for people, in a people-centered business such as public service, any initiative is doomed to fail. In order to build a successful and inspirational environment for process improvement to thrive, you must incorporate genuine respect. If it isn't genuine, people will feel that, and it won't work."

COUNTERMEASURE TO *MURI*: JOB SECURITY

Lean principles require organizations to value their customers and their employees by following the principle of respect for people that includes understanding their need for job security. As *The Kaizen Event Planner* explains, "The Lean thinking rule of thumb is that staff will only lose their employment for two reasons: (1) poor performance, or (2) market downturns."[3]

An introductory workshop on the Shingo Model sponsored by the Greater Boston Manufacturing Partnership (GBMP) includes a short video about the successful transformation of ACE Metal Crafts. The case exemplifies the Shingo principle, "respect every individual." Before agreeing to assist ACE, Toyota advisor Scott Dickson had a requirement that "no one will lose their job by our activity."[4]

Such approaches are counterintuitive for many Western businesses and bureaucracies. Too often, employees are viewed as costs, to be minimized or eliminated; those who are essential are monitored and controlled. In *Toyota Kata*, Mike Rother explains the difference in approach of a company whose goal is to make money, compared with a company whose goal is to make quality products. He explained that "moving production to lower cost countries to reduce cost" does not improve the production process—it's simply "making waste cheaper."[5]

The topic was also addressed in *The Lean Toolbox*, acknowledging that process improvements can result in "a great temptation to lay off any labor that has been saved by Lean. However, doing this even once means that Lean will be perceived as a headcount reduction tool within your operation, and no one will 'improve themselves out of a job.'"[6]

Job security and respect for employees was at the core of the Lean initiative at New Balance, the only shoe company that makes athletic shoes in the USA. The company successfully reduced the time to make a pair of shoes from 8 days in 2004, to 2 hours. Freed capacity of associates was redeployed within the company, including painting the facility and training as Lean champions.[7]

Recall the assurances provided by DOS Commissioner John Barthelmes – that jobs may change, but no one will lose their livelihood due to a Lean project. Holding to that commitment gives DOS employees the confidence to participate in improvement teams.

COUNTERMEASURE TO *MURI*: CULTURE OF INNOVATION

Concern about potential layoff is not the only source of fear. Traditional management can create a culture of blaming and shaming. In that environment, the best way to get along is to keep your head down. Since Lean needs employees fully engaged in problem solving, Lean managers know they must reward risk more than they punish failure. The PDCA cycle requires a series of experiments as the new process is validated. A Lean organization makes it safe to experiment.

Sam McKeeman cautioned that it takes 7 years for the typical employee to get beaten down and stop offering ideas. As Bert Teeuwen noted, "If unsolicited advice and creative improvement ideas go unappreciated by their managers, public servants tend to develop into individuals who just do their job on automatic pilot."[8]

City manager Dan Fitzpatrick explained, "When originally developed by Dr. Deming, there were not 14 tenets. While working with the Japanese in the 1950s, there was no need for tenets 8—Drive Out Fear—and 9—Break Down Barriers. These were developed later, when Dr. Deming applied his teachings to the United States." Urging managers to apply Deming's lessons, Fitzpatrick explained, "We must drive out fear and enable our staff and ourselves to make mistakes...Dr. Deming preached that secure employees were more effective and efficient...Workers must be able to ask questions, report accidents, and try new methods with the confidence that their superiors will back them up."[9]

Conversely, the toxic effect of "gotcha" management style also carries risk of public shaming. Weak administrators may humiliate subordinates, "throwing them under the bus" to curry favor with politicians who seek press coverage by scapegoating public employees. The Results Washington team understood both the morale impact and the practical cost of such a system. In a climate of fear, employees are unlikely to report problems.

Understanding that "you cannot solve what you do not know about" the team the team set a goal to "create a safe climate for people to surface problems." Realizing that "risk-taking invites the possibility of failure and also due to the negative publicity it can invite…they tackled head-on the fear of a 'gotcha' mentality. They promoted a culture of celebrating those who surfaced problems and solved them, rather than trying to ignore them."[10]

If the culture genuinely changes, even the most cynical employees can rally. Individual employees, supervisors and managers can play a critical role in modeling new behaviors and helping to move the culture.

COUNTERMEASURE TO *MURI*: IDEALISM AND MOTIVATION

Some managers claim that they can't address bureaucratic dysfunction because they can't give cash bonuses to individual public employees. It's a common misconception. Deming's position against rewarding individuals is backed up by others who have studied the subject.

Deming explained, "The idea of a merit rating is alluring. The sound of the words captivates the imagination: pay for what you get; get what you pay for; motivate people to do their best, for their own good. The effect is exactly the opposite of what the words promise. Everyone propels himself forward, or tries to, for his own good, on his own life preserver. The organization is the loser."[11]

Simon Sinek explored the subject in *Leaders Eat Last*. He stressed the importance of building a culture where people work for the common good and warned against organizations that pit employees against one another. He explained that such an environment causes people "to veer away from doing 'the right thing' in favor of doing 'the thing that's right for me."[12]

Bureaucratic performance can't be improved by individuals—these processes are part of a system and must be tackled systemically. Lean brings out the best in employees by creating the opportunity to for us to produce the best value for our customers and for the public. Sam McKeeman urged us to realize that the happiest employees are those who are challenged. Leaders can help to build a purpose-driven culture by respecting employees and engaging them in the shared responsibility of accomplishing the organization's mission.

COUNTERMEASURE TO *MURI:* AN EXECUTIVE CHAMPION

Our team of Lean activists really could use some "top cover" to fend off the *muri*. It would be great to have someone in charge who is willing to provide the resources and has the commitment to get things done. Even better—someone who is a Lean manager, talking the talk and walking the walk required to build a sustainable Lean culture.

The *muri* is compounded when we hear about administrators or elected officials seeking external sources to figure out how to make the organizations more efficient. The cost of developing an internal Lean team is minor compared with expenditures for consultants, who design elaborate reorganization plans, purportedly to increase efficiency. I've likened it to being a "Who" (the tiny creatures only heard by one friendly elephant in Dr. Seuss' children's book *Horton Hears a Who!*), shouting, "We are here! We are here!" Bert Teeuwen observed, "In organizations with traditional leadership...Managers are employed to solve problems and the remaining personnel perform the grunt work. When it comes to solving problems, managers in the public sector sometimes put more faith in subcontracted staff then in their own."[13]

Understanding our frustration, Dr. Darlene Dumont of the Lean Enterprise Institute (LEI) acknowledged the significant role of an executive champion to drive the cultural change and provide resources. Optimally, the Lean initiative is both top-down and bottom-up, with roles and responsibilities at all levels in the organization. She pointed to John Shook's model of the Lean house. The five dimensions include the roof – a true north of value-driven purpose—and the two pillars—process improvement and people (development of their capabilities), built on a foundation of Lean thinking and culture. Inside the house is the management system, with the leadership behaviors pulling it all together.[14]

Operationalizing Shook's model are five core questions that he describes as "fractal—meaning that the same questions apply whether working at the macro enterprise level or the level of individual responsibility as you dive progressively deeper into each dimension."[15] The five questions are:

1. What is the purpose of the change—what true north and value are we providing, or simply: what problem are we trying to solve? (the roof)
2. How are we improving the actual work? (process improvement pillar)

3. How are we building capability? (people development pillar)
4. What *leadership behaviors* and *management systems* are required to support this new way of working? (inside)
5. What basic thinking, mindset, or assumptions comprise the existing culture, and are we driving this transformation? (the foundation)[16]

What happens if the management system is not in the Lean house? What if the leadership behaviors are not supporting the culture change? *Muri* builds, as we try to compensate. It's a heavy lift just to get a program going. Will the cumulative *muri* crush us? Can we build the foundation when the inside of house is empty?

COUNTERMEASURE TO *MURI* AND *MUDA*: FULL TIME AGENCY LEAN PRACTITIONERS AND LEAN WRAP-AROUND SERVICES

New Hampshire's Department of Health & Human Services is the only agency with a process improvement staff. The two Lean Black Belts, John MacPhee and Heather Barto, don't need to do Lean on the "night shift" after their other work is done—Lean is their day job. While much remains to be done, significant progress has been made in the largest bureaucracy in the state, which has the responsibility for its most vulnerable citizens. The agency's staff suffers from *muri*, following continuous waves of budget cuts and hiring freezes. Taking the time to do Lean projects is seldom easy because people are stretched so thin. Doing a project just to learn about Lean is not the optimal model. Learning Lean by doing a project can give people hope that they can bust through the *muda* and their time can be redeployed to mission-driven work.

Heather is committed to making Lean work at DHHS, noting, "We are here because our leadership believes in process improvement now and what we can do for our services to the public." She explains, "I really enjoy connecting dots with people to process…we are able to experience that 'aha!' moment where change is possible, and improvement is found. The program's success is our success. We are fortunate to have this kind of relationship with our programs and teams. Teams know when the Lean Team is asked to work with a group, it's a help and not a hindrance. We approach each project a high level of respect for the way work is completed, observe, perform *gemba* walks, and take the time to understand root causes. The relationships we form with program staff are critical to process improvement work." (Figure 10.1).

When Heather reached out to units within DHHS, she prepared employees to bring real workplace projects to Yellow Belt training. She observed, however, that the trainees' plans for a future state for their project would often fail to be implemented after class ended and they returned to their regular duties. Realizing that both the trainees and their managers are new to Lean, she identified the need for continuity and designed a model for post-training follow-up. To improve the odds of success for Lean trainees and project teams at DHHS, Heather launched a comprehensive Lean Wrap Around Service Model in 2017.

The innovative Wrap Around Service Model starts before a group attends Lean training and follows them through to completion of their project. Heather identifies areas within the agency that could benefit from a Lean effort and works with employees and managers to register the teams for Yellow Belt training. Prior to the training, she meets with the project team to help them identify an appropriate project and prepare a draft charter. She may attend the program with the team, as their facilitator, or identify another facilitator to work with them. Following the sell and the approval of the implementation plan, Heather continues to work with the team, helping them prepare their A3 report and track their project's implementation. She is available to assist if they hit a snag in their plan, and to help them document and celebrate their gains.

Looking at the big picture, Heather observes, "As a state, we need to work with teams, teach the tools, and serve as a mentor to help reach the

FIGURE 10.1
Lean Black Belt Heather Barto, M.S, Process Improvement Specialist at NH DHHS.

end goal. It's a continual loop that is ever-growing. Like a small garden, we need to prepare the soil, replant the seeds, and take care to water to ensure the correct growing environment. Foundational work and support pays for itself in the long run. We are not a one-and-done project model at DHHS. It's more of one component done 'check' and then we ask 'what is next and what can we do about it'. We are striving to be a leader in continuous process improvement together."

Heather's work with DHHS is an important countermeasure against the *muda* of failure to launch. Elsewhere, Lean practitioners are integrating project management principles into their implementation and sustainment plans.

COUNTERMEASURE TO *MURI*: RALLY THE NIGHT SHIFT AND PROCEED UNTIL APPREHENDED

Lean activists are willing to go rogue at times. Recall Roberta's motto, "proceed until apprehended." The energy level required to live by that maxim is tough to sustain—but not impossible.

Dr. Dumont expanded on the significance of what LEI founder Jim Womack termed the "night shift." She observed, "From their organizational structures to their allotted resources, the very nature of government agencies can inhibit their lean transformation efforts. Yet there are many lean leaders in government doing small pockets of great things within their own departments, and agencies. Many of these CPI efforts are driven by internal 'volunteers' that have a passion for trying to make things better. This passion and change-agent role that they play is above and beyond their 'regular' job."[17]

Absent the role of executive champion, Dr. Dumont noted that it will take longer to build the Lean initiative than if we had both top down and bottom up efforts underway. It's not impossible though, she explained, because the behaviors and protocols can start at the lower levels. She encouraged us to build communities of practice, share our training resources, and pursue learning through the existing wealth of knowledge in the wide Lean community, including LEI and the Gemba Academy. The PDCA model of a series of small experiments can bring our initiatives forward in the manner best suited for our organizations.

I was encouraged that Dr. Dumont confirmed that we took the right path by building our community of practice and challenging ourselves to deepen our expertise. Is this model replicable for organizations that lack an executive champion and strategic plan for Lean? Perhaps understanding what drives us may be useful for constructing a sustainable Lean organization, so the next section explores the motivation of public sector Lean practitioners.

COUNTERMEASURE TO *MURI*: LEANIAC SOLIDARITY

Can *muri* be overcome without a Lean management system? Let's examine how innovative thinkers got as far as we did through a series of workarounds. Despite the collage of skills and personalities, our team of Lean activists shares a passion for our work. As the case study about Result Washington quoted Deputy Director Rich Roesler, "The real secret sauce in Lean is collaboration." He also notes that "working across agencies broadens perspectives and opens up a diversity of ideas."[18]

LEC Chair John MacPhee has described us as a volunteer army: "We are innovative, collaborative, and highly motivated to share best practices, advance the culture of Lean, and improve public performance." As Lean Black Belt Lt. Jeff Ladieu explained, "We're all here because of our work ethic and our passion."

Black Belt instructor Michael Moranti observed, "We're doing Lean because we like it. No one asked us to do it. That doesn't happen in private industry."

This spirit is not unique to New Hampshire. Public sector Lean practitioners across the country are extraordinarily dedicated to mission. Connecticut's Alison Fisher, a leader in the regional Lean network, is one such example. Alison explained,

> "I always felt that I could do more to serve the public with the resources I was given. My first exposure to Lean principles/tools was the first time I had words and concepts to describe what I wanted to do. It was easier for me to ask for supervisory approval to tackle process improvement, once I had the right vocabulary and a methodology to do it!"

The morale impact of participation in process improvement is often underestimated. A commentary in *Governing Magazine* noted: "Most public-sector workers are amazing people who came to their careers in hopes of making a difference in the lives of the people in their counties, cities, and states. We want to help the poor, protect the environment, and keep our kids safe and healthy. Often what demotivates us are the same things that upset our customers—paperwork, red tape, long lines, endless bureaucracy...When we reduce these factors in order to improve a process...we remove the demotivation that seems to grind us down over time."[19]

Once these employees are "bitten by the Lean bug," they seek additional training to enhance their skills and opportunities to conduct meaningful projects. These committed Lean practitioners build internal capacity for the organization. There are several other advantages, according to Bert Teeuwen: "Choose for the role of embedded Lean practitioners people who are good or can be good at enthusing others. They possess the skills to notice signs of resistance, overcome these, and to get the most from the teams. These are competencies other than making a good value stream map."[20]

What draws employees to become Lean activists? Given the diverse assembly of skills and qualities among our New Hampshire Lean practitioners, I thought a questionnaire might identify some common themes. The following section considers the human dimension of how and why these folks were drawn to Lean. Participants included Lean Coordinators Dan Hrobak (Environmental Services), Diane Dawson (Revenue), Edie Chiasson (Lottery), Heather Barto (Health & Human Services; Lean Executive Committee Vice Chair), and Candice Weingartner (Information Technology).

> Recall your first introduction to Lean or Lean training session. Were you converted immediately? If so, what was it about Lean that hooked you?

Dan: "I was immediately interested in Lean. I was first exposed in 2012, when my coworkers were starting to participate in Lean events. Some of these coworkers participated in other positions they held outside the state agency. These coworkers spoke about how Lean could be applied to state government. Prior to any other introduction, the opportunity came up for me to participate in a Lean event at a large manufacturing facility for a full week. I was the invited as a participant with no knowledge in the process being reviewed, also known as 'fresh eyes.'

I really enjoyed this experience, as we obtained a better understanding of the process and developed ways to improve it. We also quantified those improvements. It was a very structured way of problem solving and, from this experience, I felt that I could bring something back to my place of work."

Diane: "My first experience with Lean was in 2011 when I was approached by the DRA assistant commissioner to participate in a 3-day Lean event to be held here at the department and facilitated by Kate McGovern. The project to be leaned was our Meals & Rentals License renewal process, which was quite a bit cumbersome at best. At the onset of this event, I wasn't sure what or where we were heading, but soon realized that this process of mapping current and future state opened our eyes and minds, and we soon realized that with the right Lean tools the possibilities were endless. By the time we completed our future state, I was completely hooked on Lean! I couldn't wait to move on to the next project. It was at that moment that I decided to jump in the deep end of the Lean Pool and continue my education by becoming a process improvement practitioner and facilitator."

Edie: "My first exposure to Lean was as a participant in a project. The project was to redesign an application used at the Department of Safety— Division of Motor Vehicles. My focus as a manager for many years was to improve efficiencies and control expenses, so the concept is not new. The hook for me was recognizing Lean as a movement. Lean tools are defined, packaged, and taught so that a network/community can learn and share a language that motivates workers and ultimately benefits taxpayers."

Heather: "My first introduction to Lean thinking was during a NH Certified Public Manager training offered by the NH Bureau of Education and Training. Immediately the instructor (Kate) referenced being "bitten by the Lean bug," change champions, and went on to describe early use of Lean in the private sector. The cogwheels in my brain were immediately thinking about state government application and possible use. It was instantaneous of a 'Lean bug' and thankfully it was the kind of bite you want more of. Lean has added a formal model to the way I was already approaching problems innately. The framework works because it's simple, relatable, and has proven success. Now there is a good business reason to support my questioning 'why' on a continual basis."

> What was your favorite project? Your most successful project? What worked well and why?

Dan: "My favorite project that we worked on was on improving the inspection reporting process in the Air Resources Division at NHDES.

This program at NHDES had metrics beforehand and after, unlike many of the projects conducted at that organization. Therefore, we could see the actual improvements. We made several recommendations to improve the process. One of the things I like best was the strong facilitation and focusing on the task at hand. We achieved what we had wanted to and enjoyed the process overall."

Edie: "My favorite and most successful project was the 'Who's on First' project. It was a project to redesign the NH Lottery Commission's daily tracking/reporting of staff attendance/absences. It worked well because everyone in the agency wanted improvement on the existing process. Everyone was respectful, thoughtful, creative, proactive, and engaged."

Heather: "It's hard to select a favorite project because they are all different and have provided valuable insight. We are so lucky to get to know all the programs across the department through the Lean services we provide. One program stands out in particular because of their successful and supportive team dynamics, which was evident early on in the process. The project work looked at the start of case workflow when as it arrives in the department and its subsequent steps. The program was already advanced in terms of employee investment, management of issues, and finding early leaders, essentially has been a bonus round for me to work with. I often told the group, 'This is the gold star' kind of team that every facilitator wants to work with. This project is still in process and not yet complete. I have full faith that this program will implement sustainable process flow changes."

> What was your least favorite, or least successful project? What did you learn from it?

Dan: "I was only employed by this agency for about half of the eight or nine years that Lean has been in use. I think all the projects we had were successful. While some were not implemented as well as they could have been, we were still able to obtain lessons learned from these projects. Nothing goes 100% to plan. If I could go back, I would have done at least some things differently in each of the projects I have worked on."

Diane: "We have a few processes that were put through a *kaizen* event, not once, but three times before we had some success to show. In these instances, the important lesson learned was that we can't always have a 'winning event.' Sometimes we need to relook at a process or series of processes in order to be successful. In these instances, it was necessary to break out the processes by changing our bookends and perform events on each separate part of the whole in order to come up with a solution. It is okay to fail the first time around—we sometimes can bite off more than we can chew in our enthusiasm to 'fix' a problem; slowing down and rethinking are lessons learned that will only benefit us all and does not mean mistakes were made and can't be undone; it only means that we continue to try, maybe with a different approach, and never give up."

Edie: "I was in the role of 'fresh eyes' on my least favorite project. The facilitators of that project allowed the participants to spend hours rehashing information. There was a disturbing display of disrespect and belittling of participants by one of the facilitators. The experience gave me an opportunity to observe and be reflective about my values and form my own style of facilitating.

Also, in my experience, all Lean projects have an element of success. If nothing else, awareness is created. More often than not, a dialogue begins because light shines on an issue. It's a start and, if not addressed immediately, a seed is planted. Those are the opportunities to introduce 'phase I' and use PDCA (Plan–Do–Check–Act) as strategy to move forward with other phases."

Heather: "I think the first Lean project is always the hardest because of several aspects. It's basically a learning moment and time to reflect on your skills as a facilitator, uptake on Lean, and assessment if the team has a culture that supports process change. When we started Lean in public health, we were paving the way to creating a standardized process from scratch. Thankfully, there were seasoned facilitators from our colleagues at the Department of Safety, and others within the Department of Health and Human Services who served as side consultants. These facilitator relationships are the building blocks we have used to improve the Lean process improvement service and delivery models. The community of practice built within our Lean Network continues to be a source of mentoring, sharing information, and collaborations.

Takeaway lessons from a first project out of the gate are to assess readiness for change with a team, be ready to apply flexible facilitator styles for groups as it's not a cookie-cutter approach, and meet the team where they are at. It's also okay to halt a project and take a pause. If a team is not in a place of adopting change, we as Lean facilitators may not be as efficient as we can. The culture has to support process improvement at every level for it to work and flow for a viable business analysis tool. Much of these lessons learned during and after the project helped inform some best practices for our team."

> Lean has evolved since we started in 2009. Compare what we knew then to what we know now. Discuss your role and the contributions you have made to Lean's evolution in NH. What are you most proud of? Is there anything you would go back and change if you could?

Dan: "I started my Lean journey in 2012, so the first three years, I was not involved…I am currently involved in the statewide Lean Executive Committee, representing NHDES. I am proud that we have a charter signed by the Governor in 2017. It gives us more credibility and authority to conduct statewide Lean tasks. I am also proud of the relationships we have developed across the country. Many states have strong Lean or continuous improvement programs. NH, with a lack of a centralized office, is comparable to them in terms of what we accomplish through training, projects and outreach.

I would have tried to get a Lean endorsement or office early on. I think these attempts were made, but, for a variety of reasons, never worked out. I also would have created an overarching charter and plan from the beginning. This plan would have our goals and objectives."

Edie: "My role in Lean is multidimensional—fresh eyes, subject matter expert, facilitator, sponsor, mentor, black belt, agency coordinator, executive committee member, and cheerleader. My contributions are in supporting education, encouraging agency participation, and lobbying for an executive order to create an Office of Lean. I am most proud of my own determination. Even though I consistently experience resistance and setbacks, I am able to regroup, be proactive, and be persistent."

Heather: "Reflection is continually occurring for all of us in process improvement. It's a button I can't turn off in my brain. Essentially, those of us who work in process improvement have some hardwiring with how to approach a process and help others understand possible root causes. If we could go back, I would invite more people on this Lean ship and market the homegrown structure more. We need to continue building the network with Lean awareness and facilitation expertise. To do that we need more people trained, facilitators, and mentors. When we tell the project successes and lessons learned, we move away from "I" and then go into "we" mode for cross culture building. The more the merrier involvement and inclusion with Lean into everyday work!"

Candice: "This Lean journey has provided me with the tools and skills to assist in making a difference for the citizens of the state of NH. I find the best approach is to never be afraid to question the process and facilitate change. Some along the way might embrace change like a porcupine; however, the end game is worth the quilling."

> If you could pick one thing that management in your agency or elected leaders could do to move Lean forward, what would it be?

Dan: "I would ask management to authorize Lean as a focal point of strategic planning. In this way, we could ensure that we make the best use of our resources by creating the most effective processes to achieve our mission."

Edie: "I don't believe Lean will move forward in our state of New Hampshire government unless or until there is a mandate from the governor. I am hopeful that our elected leaders will, at some point, understand the fiscal and goodwill benefits of Lean. A commitment from the governor's office would create a path for education and progress throughout all our agencies."

Heather: "We all need training. That is the single point at the starting line for everyone: a required step one. After training we need to continue aiding programs to apply Lean concepts in the work place, offer an ongoing presence and engagement with our teams. We are so fortunate at DHHS to have support for training.

Moving forward at the state level would be to adopt an executive order, strategic plan, and resources. An executive order would allow for a buildup of infrastructure with an even deeper coordinated effort. A clear strategic plan would start the performance management component and move towards a structured feedback loop. Staffing an Office of Lean is really required at this point to move our government into forward thinking innovations and adoptions at every level. Our surrounding states have this in place."

> Where to next? What are your goals for the future of Lean in your organization? State-wide?

Dan: "Within our organization, we have created a Lean charter and roadmap for the next several years. This establishes the specific tasks, such as projects, training, and communication, that we would like to accomplish. It also specifies specific targets for each of these categories.

Statewide, we are still pushing for an Office of Continuous Improvement. There are many other priorities and activities that the governor and legislature pursue and are obligated to pursue. If we keep pushing for this office, when the time is right, it will come to fruition."

Edie: "My goal is to continue quietly practicing lean strategy, methods, and terminology in my agency. It is a subtle, incremental, successful, way of influencing the culture. As stated repeatedly, I hope there will be follow-up to the draft executive order that was prepared for our governor last year. We need a clear, statewide vision with cooperation and collaboration across all agencies. The practice of Lean is a fiscally responsible action for the benefit of all NH taxpayers."

Heather: "Continue developing and supporting the culture and enterprise alignment. To be effective with culture change it takes a dedicated team and a minimum of 3 years. We are ahead of the game in many ways but have more to do. Process improvement is an investment in the people and way we do business. It takes bravery, passion, keeping on course with a vision, creative strategy, and a true can-do attitude. We cannot do this alone, we need the change champions. For Lean statewide, we need the infrastructure to sustain continuous growth and begin looking at a global performance management structure. Enterprise alignment is critical for our strategies to be aligned and to market ourselves as a Lean-thinking and Lean-doing government. We have more to do, and I know we can do it (Figure 10.2)."

COUNTERMEASURE TO *MURI*: INNOVATION

As an impatient Lean practitioner, I was encouraged by a posting from Ken Snyder of the Shingo Institute entitled, "It Shouldn't Be This Hard."[21] Snyder challenges common assertions such as "Lean takes 10 years minimum," or "Where you start depends on where your organization is at," or "Implementing Lean is an art, not a science," as excuses "for why a transformation should take an inordinately long period of time." He argues that for the use of a scientific methodology for quicker implementation and greater levels of achievement. Influenced by the work of Malcolm Gladwell, Anders Ericson, and others, Snyder makes the case for moving away from "naïve practice" past "purposeful practice" to "deliberate practice." Using the Lean principle of standard work, the most successful Lean

FIGURE 10.2

Roberta Witham and Chris Wagner, who is now Colonel of New Hampshire State Police, with the State Police Lean Black Belt nameplates. When Commissioner Barthelmes asked Chris to go to Lean training in 2009, he was a Sergeant. In 2016, when Governor Maggie Hassan nominated him to command the State Police, Chris's biography mentioned his Lean Black Belt before his FBI Academy credential.[22]

initiatives would identify optimal training and practice techniques and implement them as rapidly as possible.

Michael Moranti had cautioned a Black Belt class about the institutional barriers presented by the siloed functions of Finance, Legal, Human Resources, and Technology. He explained, however, that these divisions could become pillars of change if you inject Innovation and Growth into the center. Then you get the acronym FLIGHT. Despite Moranti's concerns that the lack of officially recognized roles puts us at risk of being personality-dependent, he now sees substantial progress in the depth of our guerrilla movement.

We've had our bumps in the road—as in any family, there's an occasional argument. You could probably base a *Big Bang Theory*-style sitcom on the geeky things Leaniacs argue about. We're a passionate movement for public service and our commitment always moves us forward. As we hit the wall on certain aspects, we continue to seek ways around the roadblocks. We recruit others to our movement, hoping to generate a tipping point to a culture of continuous improvement, a communicable cure. As we face attrition, our ranks are replenished with new graduates of each of the Belt programs who are bringing fresh energy and creative ideas.

The innovative spirit of our Lean community is exemplified by an initiative launched in 2018. Lean Black Belt Sgt. Thomas Lencki proposed that the Lean Executive Committee (LEC) create a medallion known as a "challenge coin." As Tom explained the tradition of challenge coins in the military and in the New Hampshire State Police, LEC members enthusastically adopted the idea. The medallion will display the organization's insignia and be awarded to members of our Lean community to recognize achievements and build morale and cohesion.

One of our veteran practitioners recently reminded me that as you're climbing the mountain, every now and then, it's good to look back and enjoy the view—a valuable perspective.

Taking stock of our progress: The purposeful networking is connecting practitioners across agencies, facilitator swaps are increasingly common, and the mentorship system is taking hold. We are confident that each new class of Green and Black Belts will join in building the ties of common cause that will allow our movement to survive turnover of the founding activists.

SUMMARY OF LESSONS LEARNED

- Establish an Office of Lean to provide cross-silo coordination. The Lean office should report to the state's chief operating officer or the top administrative official, with sufficient resources that enterprise alignment becomes achievable.

- Without top-level leadership and a central Lean office to coordinate, the efforts will be uneven. Silos with a combination of management support and dedicated Lean practitioners will be more successful that those without. However, they won't be able to tackle significant cross-silo *muda*.
- Lacking the top leadership, Lean can grow as a bottom-up movement within the progressive silos. These departments can be petri dishes, experimenting with best practices and building proof of concept. Wins can be significant for the customers of those silos. The jury is still out on how long bottom-up can last without partnership from the top of the organization.
- Deming's Points #13 and #14 tell us to "institute a vigorous program of education and self-improvement," and to "put everybody in the company to work to accomplish the transformation. The transformation is everybody's job."[23] Therefore, the Lean initiative must assure equal access to training for employees working in all sections of the organization.
- Provide a multi-tier training program that incorporates theory and practice with hands-on skill application. Reinforce growth using mentoring, continuing educations, critical self-reflection, and opportunities to apply the learning.
- Top management should publish a resolution that no one will lose his job for contribution to quality and productivity.[24]

(Deming)

- Build the community of practice, both within your state and beyond. As Results Washington's Rich Roesler said, "We steal ideas from other states and welcome people to steal our ideas."[25]
- Be innovative. Continuous improvement through PDCA. *The Lean Toolbox* quotes George Box: "All models are wrong, but some models are useful."[26]

The graphic that follows depicts the dynamic model. On one path, there is a pyramid of learning built on a foundation of broad understanding by White Belts. Those who become Yellow Belts may go on to become Green Belts, and some will become Black Belts. The second path is the responsibility to bring others along. Black Belts mentor new Black Belts and developing Green Belts; Green Belts facilitate project teams in Yellow Belt classes and encourage Yellow Belts to go on to become Green Belts (Figure 10.3).

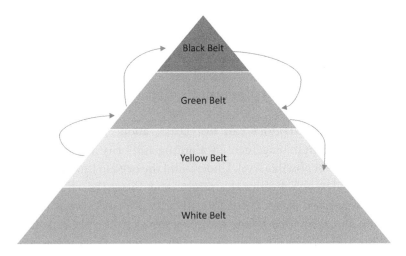

FIGURE 10.3
A dynamic model for Lean learning, mentorship and engagement.

Develop target ratios to build organizational capacity. Use PDCA to adjust your target ratios as appropriate. For example:

- Lean White Belt or Lean 101—online class for the entire workforce
- Lean for Leaders workshop for all administrators, conducted in each management team
- Yellow Belt training for at least 25% of employees in each agency
- Green Belt training a minimum ratio of 2:100 employees, with a minimum of two per agency

APPLYING THE LESSONS

- **What the governor can do**: Learn about Lean management. Issue an executive order requiring all agencies to participate in a Lean initiative focused on furthering the articulated goals and priorities for the state and assure that there will be no layoffs due to the initiative. Establish a central office for Lean and identify its authority and responsibility. Work with the legislature to develop a budget that includes the Lean office and appropriate resources so that agencies all have equal access to training. Hold agencies accountable for their responsibility to participate.

- **What legislators can do**: Learn about Lean. Provide resources for a state office of Lean, accessible training, and guarantee no layoffs due to Lean initiatives. Allow agencies keep 20% of documented savings for future budgets. Assist in the removal of antiquated legal restrictions and other monuments of *muda* by taking appropriate legislative action.

- **What administrators can do**: Learn about Lean management. Practice Lean management by aligning authority and responsibility at the lowest possible level. Understand the need to link *kaizen* events to broader organizational strategy and focus the efforts accordingly. Assign Lean coordinators, identify priority projects that align with the agency's mission, assign sponsors to the projects, provide resources, and require follow-through. Reiterate that there will be no layoffs due to Lean projects. Do daily *gemba* walks. Ask how you can help the employees succeed.

- **What managers and supervisors can do**: Learn about Lean management. Sponsor Lean projects. Assign Lean project teams. Facilitate the participation by all appropriate team members by modifying schedules and job duties, if necessary. Practice Lean management by aligning authority and responsibility at the lowest possible level. Do daily *gemba* walks. Ask how you can help the employees succeed.

- **What all staff can do**: Learn about Lean and how to apply it. Understand *kaizen* as a concept in furtherance of organizational excellence, and how *kaizen* events empower employees to reduce waste and add value. Help to identify projects and participate on teams. Build Lean culture every day through continuous improvement activities and ongoing responsibility for excellent customer service.

- **What Lean activists can do**: Continually learn more about Lean and apply it in practice. Facilitate projects, document gains. Promote best practices. Mentor new Lean practitioners, model behaviors of continuous improvement, and spread Lean culture. Develop collaborative models including cross-silo facilitator swaps, and participation as guest faculty in training programs. Create a broad community of practice and a thriving community of excellence. Proceed until apprehended. Keep innovating. Live Lean and prosper.

IN CLOSING

The lessons captured here from this stage of our journey are by no means exhaustive. There are lots of other tools and techniques to learn and many innovations yet to come. In dozens of states across the country, this story is playing out somewhat differently. We seek to learn from one another with humility and respect. Synthesize, improve, adapt, collaborate.

Sam McKeeman quotes the proverb: What's the best time to plant an oak tree? 20 years ago. What's the second-best time? Now.

Consider the prediction from Womack, Jones, and Roos in 1990: "In this process we've become convinced that the principles of lean production can be applied equally in every industry across the globe and that the conversion to lean production will have a profound effect on human society—it will truly change the world."[27]

NOTES

1 Ken Miller, *Extreme Government Makeover: Increasing our Capacity to Do More Good* (Governing Books, a Division of Governing Magazine, 2011) 10.

2 John Bicheno and Matthias Holweg, *The Lean Toolbox 5th Edition* (PICSIE Books, Buckingham, England, 2016) 40.

3 Karen Martin and Mike Osterling, *The Kaizen Event Planner* (CRC Press, Taylor & Francis Group, LLC, Boca Raton, FL, 2007) 90.

4 Steve James, "116 Innovators," October 1, 2015, The Toyota Effect. Accessed March 28, 2018. www.youtube.com/watch?v=jga9-pFPI0M.

5 Mike Rother, *Toyota Kata* (McGraw-Hill Education, 2010) 68.

6 John Bicheno and Matthias Holweg, *The Lean Toolbox 5th Edition* (Picsie Books, 2016) 101.

7 Raye Wentworth, Keynote Speaker, Lean Systems Summit, Portland, Maine (August 9–10, 2018) 6. Program book Accessed August 11, 2018. http://files.constantcontact.com/bc5913ae501/2156d9fc-84a5-443a-be8d-64f11d9c62da.pdf.

8 Bert Teeuwen, *Lean for the Public Sector: The Pursuit of Perfection in Public Service* (Taylor& Francis Group, LLC, Productivity Press, New York, 2011) 27.

9 Daniel W. Fitzpatrick, *Deming in Local Government*, Public Sector Network: A Division of the American Society for Quality, Winter 2000, Vol. 5, No. 2.

10 Jane Wiseman, "Case Study: Performance Management and Lean Process Improvement—Results Washington, An Operational Excellence Government Success Story," Harvard Kennedy School, July 2017 (26). Accessed March 21, 2018. www.innovations.harvard.edu/opex/research/case-study-performance-management-and-lean-process-improvement-results-washington.

11 The W. Edwards Deming Institute, W. Edwards Deming Quotes. Accessed May 15, 2018. http://quotes.deming.org/authors/W._Edwards_Deming/quote/1003.

12 Simon Sinek, *Leaders Eat Last: Why Some Teams Pull Together and Others Don't* (Penguin Random House, LLC, New York, 2014, 2017) 162.

13 Bert Teeuwen, *Lean for the Public Sector: The Pursuit of Perfection in Public Service* (Taylor & Francis Group, LLC, Productivity Press, New York, 2011) 75.

14 John Shook Explains the Lean Transformation Model, The Lean Enterprise Institute, Published on You Tube, Jan 21, 2014. Accessed May 17, 2018. www.youtube.com/watch?v=kEcdliWZH30.

15 John Shook, Transforming Transformation, Posted January 22, 2014 on The Lean Enterprise Institute Blog. Accessed May 18, 2018. www.lean.org/shook/DisplayObject.cfm?o=2533.

16 Joshua Rapoza, A Lean Transformation Model Everyone Can Use, Posted January 23, 2014 on The Lean Enterprise Institute Blog. Accessed May 18, 2018. www.lean.org/LeanPost/Posting.cfm?LeanPostId=135.

17 Darlene Dumont, Ph.D., "Towards a More Perfect (i.e. Lean) Union," Posted by Lean Enterprise Institute October 28, 2015. www.lean.org/LeanPost/Posting.cfm?LeanPostId=493 accessed February 22, 2018.

18 Jane Wiseman, "Case Study: Performance Management and Lean Process Improvement—Results Washington, An Operational Excellence Government Success Story," Harvard Kennedy School, July 2017 (27). Accessed March 21, 2018. www.innovations.harvard.edu/opex/research/case-study-performance-management-and-lean-process-improvement-results-washington.

19 Governing Magazine, The Unintended Consequences of Improvement, November 11, 2013. www.governing.com/columns/smart-mgmt/The-Unintended-Consequences-of-Improvement.html.

20 Bert Teeuwen, *Lean for the Public Sector: The Pursuit of Perfection in Public Service* (Taylor & Francis Group, LLC, Productivity Press, New York, 2011) 85.

21 Ken Snyder, It Shouldn't Be This Hard, Posted on the Shingo Blog December 11, 2017. https://blog.shingo.org/2017/12/it-shouldnt-be-this-hard/.

22 Carol Robidoux, "Hassan Gives Nod to Capt. Christopher Wagner as New State Police Director," September 20, 2016. Accessed April 23, 2018. https://manchesterinklink.com/hassan-gives-nod-capt-christopher-wagner-new-state-police-director/.

23 "Dr. Deming's 14 Points for Management," The Deming Institute. Accessed February 13, 2018. https://deming.org/explore/fourteen-points.

24 The W. Edwards Deming, *Out of Crisis* (26). The Deming Institute webpage. Accessed May 19, 2018. http://quotes.deming.org/authors/W._Edwards_Deming/quote/10208.

25 Jane Wiseman, "Case Study: Performance Management and Lean Process Improvement—Results Washington, An Operational Excellence Government Success Story," Harvard Kennedy School, July 2017 (5). Accessed March 21, 2018. www.innovations.harvard.edu/opex/research/case-study-performance-management-and-lean-process-improvement-results-washington.

26 John Bicheno and Matthias Holweg, *The Lean Toolbox 5th Edition* (Picsie Books, 2016) 4.

27 James P. Womack, Daniel T. Jones, and Daniel Roos, *The Machine That Changed the World* (Free Press, A Division of Simon & Schuster, Inc., New York, N.Y., 1990, 2007) 6.

Appendix A: Agenda for the White Belt program

Below is the agenda for New Hampshire's online White Belt program that was posted on the Moodle site in October 2017.

RESOURCES

Welcome to Lean White Belt! This program introduces Lean process improvement techniques to public sector employees, supervisors, managers and administrators.

Lean charter template, 5 Whys and 5S worksheets, A3 templates.

INTRODUCTION AND INSTRUCTIONS

The White Belt class covers six components in four separate segments.

- Module I introduces Lean and the key concepts of customer value and waste identification.
- Module II introduces you to a core Lean tool—the *kaizen* event, followed by a description of how *kaizen* projects are organized. The module concludes with a brief overview of other Lean tools: the 5S, the 5 Whys, and the A3.
- Module III provides information about the NH Lean Network and the Lean Executive Committee, as well as examples of the use of Lean in several state agencies. The module concludes by asking you to identify possible applications of Lean in your organization.
- Module IV provides case studies of the use of Lean in NH State Agencies.

Instructions: *Print out the Charter template, the A3 template, the 5S and the 5 Whys worksheets that are posted in the Resource section of this classroom. You should also have pen and paper available for portions of the program.*

MODULE I: INTRODUCTION TO LEAN

- The definition of Lean and its applications in manufacturing and in public service
- The concept of customer value
- Identifying the Eight Wastes
- How many of the Eight Wastes can you find in "Lucy in the Chocolate Factory?" (link to YouTube film clip)

MODULE II: *KAIZEN* EVENTS AND OTHER LEAN TOOLS

- Description of the steps in a basic *kaizen*
- Overview of other Lean tools

MODULE III: USING LEAN IN STATE GOVERNMENT

A brief narrated PowerPoint program describing the statewide effort. (Trainers should post the charter or executive order as reference documents.)

MODULE IV: LEAN BY AGENCY

Instructions: Select one of the agency case studies from the list below. This section is intended to prepare you to join Lean events in your agency or help to start a Lean team if your agency doesn't already have one!

(Trainers should ask the Lean coordinator in each agency to provide a case study to be posted in Module IV, along with contact information, so the new Lean White Belts can connect with the agency's efforts.)

Appendix B: Training Exercise for a Yellow Belt Class

This hypothetical project can be used during a Yellow Belt class if participants have not brought a real project from their workplace. Participants will be assigned roles in the process for obtaining permission to travel out of state. Working as a team, they will map the current state, establish the metrics, design a future state, and present their findings to the project sponsor.

Learning objectives for the exercise:

- To apply Lean tools of process mapping and the 5 Whys
- To recognize and reduce the wastes of waiting and underutilized human talent
- To apply the Lean principles of aligning authority and responsibility at the lowest possible level

Background on the travel permission process: All employees must complete the A24 form to receive permission to travel out of state. The form must be signed by as many as six people, in different roles within the agency hierarchy. Supplemental instructions sent in early 2018 informed staff that they should allow six weeks for the process to be completed, including two weeks for the request to be considered by the commissioner's office, and one week "just in case the request gets held up anywhere in the approval process." They were also instructed to add half of the cost of the quote to "buffer any difference between the quoted fare and the actual fare that will be paid."

Instructions to the trainer:

- Identify a Lean facilitator to guide the project team. Assign roles for the team members. Note: this project will lose impact if the group ignores the dynamics of role and rank and tries to do collective problem solving, so remind them to stay in character. It will help to use

***Kaizen* Event Charter for Out-of-state Travel**	
Opportunity statement: *Process description & business case for the project*	The governor has asked for a 10% reduction in the amount of time DHHS spends on paperwork, and that he will no longer be reviewing requests for out of state travel. Commissioner Keegan has agreed to sponsor a Lean event to reduce the paperwork internal to the agency
Problem statement: *In the form of a question starting with "How"*	How do we reduce the paperwork for the out-of-state travel process, while assuring that the travel is professionally appropriate, and costs are covered by the current budget?
Project scope and boundaries: *The first and last steps in the process*	From the time the traveler makes the request to the point travel is approved
Key performance indicators: *time, money, quality*	Time: Reduction of time by 10% Money: Expenses must not exceed allocated budgets Quality: Send the appropriate staff to the professionally relevant trainings and conferences
Anticipated barriers	Risk-averse administrators, administrators unfamiliar with the travel budgets
Resources available	Time of the team
Customer: *End user*	Traveler
Stakeholders	Local health officials seeking guidance on protocols for dealing with these viruses, the public seeking protection from these viruses
Team Members	
Team leader: *Champion/ project manager*	Heather Barlow, Bureau Chief, Bureau of Disease Control
Core team: *Name and title of each member in the process*	Sara Jones, Epidemiologist; Tyler Bradshaw, Section Administrator for Communicable Diseases; Heather Barlow, Bureau Chief, Bureau of Disease Control; Dr. Jonathan Smith, Division Director of Public Health Services; Jane Doe, Finance Administrator
Data manager: Fresh eyes	Optional: Add an employee from another agency as "fresh eyes" who will assist the team by asking "why" questions—a participant in the class could play himself/herself
Customer(s) and/or stakeholder(s)	Optional: Add a local town health official who is relying on guidance from this program, or a member of the public concerning about contracting one of the viruses
Sponsor (name/title)	Commissioner Peter Keegan

name tents, so the facilitator is prompted to address them using their characters' names.

- Explain that this is just a training exercise, and the team will use data from a single case to map the current state of the process and design a future state. Real projects will use more data, with input from multiple customer experiences, prior to developing appropriate countermeasures to lean the process.

ROLES

Sara Jones, Epidemiologist. Sara is a new hire at the Division of Public Health Services. Her position is funded by a grant, which includes funding for attendance at professional seminars, so she can keep current in her field. She is requesting permission to attend a conference at the Center for Disease Control (CDC) in Atlanta, scheduled to precede the season of primary exposure to mosquito transmitted illnesses such as Zika and West Nile Virus.

Tyler Bradshaw, Section Administrator for Communicable Diseases. Tyler knows that the incidence of tropical diseases has been increasing in recent years, and Sara's expertise is critical for the agency's ability to understand the nature of the threat to public health. He is also very supportive of Sara's professional development plan to become increasingly more proficient in her field.

Heather Barlow, Bureau Chief, Bureau of Disease Control. Heather prepared the grant application to fund a new epidemiologist position because she was concerned about the uptick in mosquito borne illnesses. She was delighted when grant was awarded, and hired Sara Jones, a very qualified candidate. She is confident that Sara will gain important information from CDC, including the opportunity to discuss the challenges with colleagues from other states.

Dr. Jonathan Smith, Division Director of Public Health Services. Shares the concerns of Bureau Chief Barlow. He is frustrated because of the staff time consumed by the signature process and concerned that the agency will not be fully prepared with the most current medical information about disease transmissions if Sara is unable to attend the upcoming conference.

Jane Doe, Finance Administrator. Jane is required to provide financial information on the form, even though the conference was fully funded by the grant and the bureau chief had access to the same information. She believes that it's part of her job to authorize all spending because the staff might make mistakes, which would be difficult to correct after the money has been spent.

Peter Keegan, Commissioner. Commissioner Keegan is a reluctant sponsor. He is not on the team, but the information the team receives about workflow makes it clear that the commissioner currently has a role in the process. A trainer can play the role of Commissioner Keegan during the "sell" (project presentation).

Optional: Add at least one employee from another agency as "fresh eyes" who will assist the team by asking "why" questions—a participant in the class could play himself/herself. Add a customer—perhaps a local town health official who is relying on guidance from this program, or a member of the public concerned about contracting one of the viruses.

Instructions to the trainer: The information below should allow the project team to map the current state process flow. It provides the actual **work time** for each of the steps conducted by the various employees throughout the process. When they convene as a team to map the process, they should have enough information to determine the **cycle time** (the work time plus the wait time intervals in between each of the steps). Participants should be creative—they can embellish the scenario as long as they stay in character.

For this exercise, use an abbreviated version of the data sheet (below). After completing the current state map, the team members should populate fields A and B for the entire process before evaluating the value (or lack of value) for each step.

Sara, the epidemiologist, completed the A24 form to request permission to attend the CDC conference. Work time for the form = 30 minutes. She hand-delivered the form to the Section Administrator in the next cubicle. Work time = 1 minute.

Tyler, the Section Administrator, is stationed in the next cubicle. He was on a webinar when Sara put the A24 on his desk, so the form waited an hour before he reviewed it. Tyler noticed that the agenda for the conference was not attached. He wrote a sticky note on the form and returned it to Sara's cubicle while she was at lunch. Work time to review and return the form = 5 minutes.

Sara returned from lunch and saw the note. She logged on to the CDC site to find the agenda, printed it and returned the form to Tyler. (Re)work time = 5 minutes.

Tyler was at his desk and confirmed that the agenda was attached. He signed the form and brought it down the hall to the office of Bureau Chief Barlow. Work time = 5 minutes.

Step name:

A. **Work time**: The actual work time to complete the task. Work time for this step

= _____

B. **Cycle time**: The time it takes to complete the step: from the end of the previous step to the end of this step—including wait times, setup time, routing time, actual work time, and any delays

Cycle time for this step = _____

Color-coded assessments of value. Green = value added; red = non-valued-added (*muda*); yellow = non-value added to the customer, but necessary to operate the business

Heather was testifying at a legislative hearing when the form reached her desk. The legislative committee asked for additional information, which required immediate follow-up work, and the form waited on her desk for 2 days. She signed the form permitting Sara Jones to travel. Work time = 5 minutes to read and sign.

Jane, the finance administrator, is required to provide financial information on the form, even though the conference was fully funded by the grant and the bureau chief had access to the same information. Jane was busy with requests from a legislative committee, so the form waited 4 days. Work time = 15 minutes to complete the information and sign the form.

Dr. Smith was busy with many urgent medical duties, so the form waited 3 days for his signature. He saw that Jane had signed off on the financial aspect, so he signed the form. Work time = 5 minutes to read and sign.

Commissioner Keegan: Denied Sara Jones' travel request because he had already approved three requests that month and he was concerned that would look bad if the press wrote a story about employees traveling to out-of-state conferences while the department was requesting a dozen new positions to protect abused children. The form waited on his desk for 5 days before he rejected the request. Work time to reject the request = 2 minutes.

Instructions to the trainer: After the team has completed the data sheets for the current state, they should tally the work time and cycle time and start the summary table.

Instructions to the trainer: The team should map the future state with the goal of eliminating steps that do not add value. Next, they complete the summary table and prepare a presentation for Commissioner Keegan, asking him to approve the new workflow. The exercise concludes with their presentation and the response by someone playing the role of Commissioner Keegan.

	Current State	Future State	% Change
Total work time (typical)			
Total cycle time (typical)			
Total # steps			
#Value-added to the customer			
#Non-valued added			
#Non-value added-necessary			

Debrief after the exercise:

- Ask the participants why they think the process is so entrenched.
- Discuss the principles of good process design, mistake-proofing, and alignment of authority and responsibility. What kind of cultural change would be required? What training?
- Share a quote from *The Lean Handbook*: "the most effective way to maximize resources is to ensure that quality (as defined by your customer) is built in...by the people doing the work...It has also been proven many times that even 100% inspection is only 80–90% effective. Quality at the source involves a cultural change."[1]

NOTE

1 Anthony Manos and Chad Vincent, Editors, *The Lean Handbook* (ASQ Quality Press, Milwaukee, WI, 2012) 71.

Appendix C: Instructions for Facilitators Leading Projects in Yellow Belt Classes

#1—Lead the team in refining a draft charter & developing ground rules

- Welcome the team to the project and explain the purpose of ground rules, using examples such as "leave rank at the door" and "no blame"
- Guide the team through the adoption of rules; post on flip chart paper
- Distribute a draft charter, and identify the project sponsor and team leader
- Gain consensus on the problem statement and the scope of the project
- Identify the end user customer and any internal customers
- Identify a data manager for an electronic template of the A3 report and another team member to post the major fields on flip chart paper (optional)
- Ask someone to write the problem statement and end-user customer on flip chart paper

#2—Preparing to map the current state

- Guide the group to set up the room, so that all team members are positioned to participate
- Identify & clarify tasks: Who will write the steps? Who will post the steps on the map?
- Explain the concept of "bright ideas" and set up a page to capture them
- Explain the color and/or shape codes for the sticky notes
- Start the mapping by identifying and posting the swim lanes

#3—Current state and data sheets

- Guide the team in completing the current state map
- Introduce the data sheets and explain work time and cycle time (the time elapsed from the end of the previous step to the end of this step—including delays, interruptions, etc.)
- Explain that for training, we estimate min/max/typical, but for a real event they should do their best to determine the actual process time and post it directly on the sticky note for each step
- Identify a team member to write on the data sheets with the team's input

#4—Value added/Non-value-added assessment

- Guide the team in categorizing each step as value-added (VA), non-value-added (NVA), or non-value-added but necessary (NVA-N). Remind the team to keep the end-user customer's perspective in mind while assessing the value of each step.
- Make it visual by adding green (VA), red (NVA), and yellow (NVA-N) dots to the data sheets. Optional: for regulatory processes, add the use of orange dots to signify value to the public.
- Ask a team member to tally the number of steps that are VA, NVA, and NVA-N.

#5—Summary metrics

- Ask a team member to add the typical work time and cycle time for all the steps in the current state.
- Convert the tally into meaningful measurements. A cycle time of hundreds of hours or thousands of minutes could be converted into work days, juxtaposed with a much briefer amount of work time. Example: This process requires 3 hours of work but takes six weeks to accomplish.
- Ask a team member to prepare the summary table on flip chart paper.

#6—Brainstorming and *Kaizen* Bursts

- Guide the team in brainstorming for the future state design by first revisiting the list of bright ideas. Invite out-of-the-box thinking to generate additional ideas.
- Focus the attention to the NVA and NVA-N steps. Discuss the root causes for the waste in the process. Use the 5 Whys and/or assign research to team members.

- Explain the use of the *kaizen* burst to signify supplemental tasks and new projects. Example: creating an online form or redoing a form to make it more user-friendly.

#7—Map the future state

- Revisit the management goals on the charter to make sure the team is within the scope of authorized work. Explain the concept of an interim state as a way to move forward. (Don't let the perfect be the enemy of the good.)
- Lift the current state map up on the wall, and post fresh mapping paper below it.
- Identify team members to write steps and post them on the map, rewriting all steps that will be retained, omitting those that will be eliminated, and re-sequencing if appropriate.
- Remind the team that it is okay to add steps for the purpose of improving flow and quality.
- Guide the team in designing the future state and including any *kaizen* bursts on the map.

#8—Metrics for future state and summary table

- Guide the team in posting the data sheets in the future state, evaluating VA/NVA steps, compiling the proposed work time and cycle time.
- Identify a team member to tally the metrics and post on them on the summary table, using consistent units of measurement to provide clear contrasts.
- Ask the data manager to include this information on the A3 report.

#9—Improvement task identification and prioritization

- Identify a team member to post the improvement task priority grid (easy to do/big improvement, etc.).
- Guide the team in identifying the tasks required to move from the current state to the future state, revisiting each of the *kaizen* bursts, and deciding appropriate priority/effort category for each task and *kaizen*.

#10—Implementation plan: Tasks, roles, and responsibilities

- Guide the team in developing the implementation plan: who will be responsible for each task, and when will it be due? Consider omitting any tasks in the "hard to do/small improvement" category and fast-tracking the "easy to do/big improvement."

- Are all the tasks within the scope of resources authorized by the sponsor in the charter?
- Discuss a communication plan—does the team anticipate resistance?
- Confirm the tasks, timeline and project management responsibilities with the champion
- Ask the data manager to include this information on the A3 report

#11—A3 report & follow-up plan

- Gain agreement from the team for the final field of the A3 report— the follow-up—how will the new work flow be sustained as standard work?
- Remind the team about PDCA—Plan, Do, Check, Act/Adjust. Who will check and confirm the implementation of the future state? Determine the schedule for team communication.
- Ask the data manager to complete the electronic copy of A3 report (optional) and another team member to post the highlights on the flip chart version.

#12—Presentation prep

- Organize the team for its presentation to the class and to the project sponsor, using the visuals to highlight the findings, conclusions and recommendations, and making sure that each member has a role.

Appendix D: Training Exercise for a Green Belt Class

This hypothetical scenario can be used to challenge Green Belt students because it includes a multi-jurisdictional legacy process. Instructions to the trainer:

- The Green Belt students will take turns facilitating different phases of a basic *kaizen*-mapping project. The other students will play the various roles of team members and rotate into the role of facilitator. They'll need to be reminded to stay in character throughout the *kaizen* event because it's very tempting to forget their assigned roles and insert their own ideas about how to solve the problem. Participants should make name tents with the names of their characters, to remind the facilitator to call them by the names of their characters.
- Select one student to be Facilitator #1—that person will rotate into every role, as each of the other students takes turns facilitating. For example, Green Belt student Patrick is Facilitator #1. He guides the team in development of ground rules and review of the charter. Next, the student playing Betsy steps up to guide the team in mapping the current state, while Patrick plays Betsy. When the student playing Tracy steps up to facilitate, Patrick will play that character, and so on.
- Use the instructions on the steps in a basic *kaizen* (Chapter 4 or in Appendix C) to segment the activities, so students will complete each activity before switching facilitation roles.
- After each participant completes his/her turn as facilitator, pause the exercise and ask the group to provide feedback. What facilitation skills did this student use? What went well? What might have been done differently? Note any lessons learned for facilitating real *kaizens* in the future.
- The information needed for the role-play includes: roles, process flow, work time, and cycle time for the various steps conducted by

the characters. Print out the blurb for each role separately for each participant and provide a copy of all roles to Facilitator #1, who will rotate into all roles.

- Each one of these characters has the information about their own step(s) in the process as DCFY attempts to hire Sarah, an applicant for the job of Child Protective Service Worker (CPSW). Note that unlike a real event, this training project will map only one scenario—the effort to hire one CPSW.
- The facilitator(s) will be asking the characters what they did and how long it took, just as in a real event. Be creative. Participants are free to make up information to fill in any blanks in the scenario, providing they stay in character.

Betsy, Hiring Manager at the Division of Children Youth and Families— Betsy is very dedicated to the mission to protect children at risk for abuse and neglect. In recent years, the opioid epidemic has made an already difficult job even more challenging. The Child Protective Service Workers (CPSWs) have a high burnout rate and Betsy has been losing sleep worrying that another child will be harmed while vacant positions remain unfilled, and that qualified candidates will take other jobs rather than wait to hear back from DHHS. She is happy because her interview team has just selected a great candidate, Sarah, to be hired to be as a new CPSW. Sarah is the best applicant she has seen in a long time. Betsy is very eager to get Sarah on board, and she's frustrated by the extra steps in the process. She did the reference check and began working on the DOP required process as soon as the interview panel agreed that Sarah should be offered the position.

Mike, HR Director at Dept. of Health & Human Services— Mike has HR experience from the private sector and is frustrated by the extra steps the State requires. He cares about the agency's customers—particularly the children and families at risk, and he is very concerned with the morale of the DHHS employees. He understands that the jobs they have are tough enough without subjecting them to administrative barriers, so he's always willing to run interference for the hiring managers.

Tracy, HR Technician at the Division of Personnel (DOP)— Tracy's job requires coverage of two units within DOP. Tracy is a natural change agent, who would normally be very skeptical of the requirement to send the structured interview scores to DOP, but she was already transferred once within the unit, and she is afraid that she'll be laid off if the process is simplified to remove DOP from the process.

Phyllis, Supervisor at DOP—Phyllis is also on the team, but not directly part of the process. (Stan, the co-sponsor, is hoping that this project will win her over, so they can comply with the governor's requirement to hire more CPSWs). Phyllis has worked at DOP for many years and knows that some staff members in agency HR units make errors. She believes that DOP's staff needs to check their work, so that errors can be corrected. She is strongly opposed to changing the requirement for structured interview scores to be sent to DOP because several years ago an HR administrator tried to cheat on points to justify giving a job to a favored candidate.

Data manager: The team should choose one of the characters to be a data manager to keep track of the charter and other event documents.

Optional roles:

Customer: Sarah, Applicant for Child Protective Service Worker—Sarah was the top choice of the interview panel. She is very eager to begin work because she knows the agency is overwhelmed by heavy caseloads, leaving many children are at risk. She loves children and will be a very dedicated CPSW. Also, Sarah really needs to get to work to pay her student loans.

Stakeholder: Dan, Police Chief in a local community—He and his officers respond to emergencies, including incidents of domestic violence involving injuries to children. They know the importance of having CPSWs available to follow-up with the families at risk—before they are called back to respond to a tragedy. Dan has been invited to join the team by his friend, Terry, who is the Director of DCYF.

Supplemental roles: Background about people who are *not* on the core *kaizen* project team, but who could be added to the role-play.

Sponsor: Stan, DOP Administrator—Wants to respond to agency concerns and simplify the process but is reluctant to order his staff make the changes. He's hoping the Lean process will allow them to see the importance of changing and make them part of the solution.

Stakeholder: Terry, DCFY Director—Tragically, several toddlers have died from abuse within the past few years, and DCYF has been approved to add positions to deal with the crisis. Terry is eager for the process to change so that qualified candidates can be hired as quickly as possible. Terry has invited his friend Dan, a local police chief, who knows how important it is to have early intervention on suspected cases of child abuse.

Caucus member: Bob, supervisor in IT—Bob's unit expended staff resources to meet the business requirements for the IT system to conduct the current process. It could take a significant investment of time and effort to undo it—pulling resources away from other projects.

Kaizen Event Charter for the Structured Interview Review Process	
Opportunity statement: *Process description & business case for the project*	The governor has asked the DHHS commissioner to fully staff the CPSW positions within 6 weeks. Several *kaizen* teams have been assigned to address the problem, including this project team, sponsored by a DOP Administrator who has agreed to eliminate DOP's role in processing the scores of structured interviews. Of the more than 2100 job titles in state service, only 67 require DOP to process interview scores
Problem statement: *In the form of a question starting with "How"*	How can the structured interview scoring process be improved, so DCYF can comply with the governor's order to fully staff the CPSWs?
Project scope and boundaries	From the time the candidate is selected to the time the offer letter is sent
Key performance indicators: *Time, money, quality*	Time & money: Reduction of staff time spent on redundant structured interview scoring, freed capacity of staff to perform other duties Quality: Hire qualified candidates
Anticipated barriers	Administrators concerned about due diligence, a staff member who fears being laid off
Resources available	Time of the team and facilitator
Customer: *End user*	Applicant
Customer: Internal	Hiring manager
Stakeholders	Abused and neglected children, local law enforcement
Team Members	
Team leader/ Project manager	Mike, DHHS HR Director
Core team	Betsy, Hiring Manager at DCYF; Mike, DHHS HR Director; Tracy, HR Technician at DOP; Phyllis, DOP supervisor
Data manager	
Fresh eyes	Optional: Add an employee from another agency as "fresh eyes" who will assist the team by asking "why" questions
Customer(s) and/or stakeholder(s)	Optional: Add a Sarah, the applicant, Terry, the DHHS administrator, or a Dan, local town police chief who relies on DCYF to remove children from harmful situations
Caucus members: *On call SMEs*	Optional: Add Bob, the supervisor of the IT unit to estimate the time required to take the DOP out of the hiring process
Facilitator(s)	
Sponsors (name/title)	Stan, the DOP Administrator

Mapping exercise: Using this single event scenario, document the current state for the process to hire CPSW Sarah. Design an improved future state.

The following information about the timing of the process should be available to all team members, but the character doing the work at each step should be the one to provide the information to the facilitator during the mapping exercise. For example, the facilitator will ask Besty what she did and how long it took, and then ask Mike what he did and how long it took.

Betsy began working on the DOP required process as soon as the interview panel agreed that Sarah should be offered the position. Work time to prep and send DOP requirements to DHHS HR Dept: Work time: 15 minutes. (The cycle time is the same as the work time since this is the first step in the scope of this Lean event).

Mike receives the scores of Sarah's structured interview. He is delighted and relieved to see such a great new CPSW ready to join the staff, and he sends the scores to Tracy at DOP. Work time: 10 minutes. Cycle time: 30 minutes.

Tracy returns from her duties covering another unit within DOP and begins her work on the accumulated requests for posting structured interview scores. She identifies an error—Mike had omitted the front page of Sarah's certified state application, which is required for those who apply on paper. Time to discover the omission and sends an email to inform Mike: Work time: 5 minutes. Cycle time: 3 days.

Mike returns from a staff meeting and sees the message from Tracy. He sends the email to Betsy, asking her to get the document. Work time: 5 minutes. Cycle time: 30 minutes.

Betsy returns from lunch and sees the message from Mike asking for the document. She opens the file, finds the document, scans it and sends it to Mike. Work time: 10 minutes. Cycle time: 1 hour.

Mike is at his desk when Betsy's message arrives, and he sends it to Tracy at DOP. Work time: 2 minutes. Cycle time: 5 minutes. Note: the rework rate for DHHS HR is about 5%; the rework rate for other agencies with smaller volume and less experience with the transaction requirements is close to 90%.

Tracy returns from her other duties in DOP and sees that Mike has sent the document. She enters the info into NHFIRST, including Sarah's structured interview scores. She notifies Mike that it's all set. Work time: 5 minutes. Cycle time: 1 day.

Mike contacts Betsy and sends the offer letter to Sarah. Work time: 10 minutes. Cycle time: 30 minutes.

Instructions to trainer: Remind the participants to stay in character. Remind them to pause to provide feedback after each student has his/her turn facilitating. Pause the exercise after two or three have had the opportunity to facilitate. Debrief by asking the facilitators and the team members to comment on the challenges—what do they think went well, how might things be handled differently?

Summary: So, what happens when rookie Lean facilitators try to run this *kaizen*? It's about 50/50. Sometimes the team agrees to eliminate the requirement to send structured interview scores to DOP, other times the team agrees to keep it intact while negotiating modest reforms. It's a challenging scenario, and a good segue into various discussions about change management, sponsors and team composition.

Appendix E: Lean Training Programs

New Hampshire Bureau of Education & Training's Lean Programs

Programs	Description
White Belt	An overview of Lean concepts and techniques preparing participants to identify opportunities for improvement projects in their organizations
Yellow Belt	A hands-on introduction to the philosophy and methodology of Lean process improvement. During the 3-day class, participants apply *kaizen* process mapping techniques to an actual work process and construct an implementation plan to enact the improvements
Green Belt	Facilitation and change management. Participants prepare to become Lean practitioners and learn how to guide a group through a *kaizen* event, while considering the challenges of organizational change. Following the 3 days of classes, students will participate in a required practicum. *Pre-requisite: Yellow Belt*
Black Belt	Participants in this ten-session program combine classroom study, mentorship and practical application. The students examine Lean principles and practices including Shingo, Kata, and Hoshin Kanri, and they conduct a capstone project to apply their skills and to understand Lean from an operational and strategic perspective. *Pre-requisites: Yellow and Green Belts; Application with personal statement and A3 report of Green Belt practicum required*
Lean Friday Forums	Continuing education sessions. *Pre-requisite: Green Belt*
Lean for Leaders	A 60–90 minute workshop that prepares directors and administrators for their role in Lean initiatives and Lean management. Available for agency management teams upon request

Green Belt: Active Status requirements	Learning: Have a mentor. Share Lean articles and insights. Attend at least one Friday Forum, Network meeting or conference Application: Facilitate or co-facilitate a *kaizen* event, prepare an A3 Report on that project and review it with your mentor Verification: Send a summary of your learning activities and insights to BET and to your agency's Lean coordinator. Attach your A3 report including any feedback from your mentor
Black Belt: Active Status requirements	Learning: Have a mentor. Share Lean articles and insights. Attend at least one Friday Forum, network meeting, or conference Application: Continuously apply your Black Belt skills to advance Lean in your organization. Use the A3 format to identify the current condition and your goals. Review it with your mentor at several stages during the year, using *Kata* Verification: Send a summary of your learning activities and insights to BET and to your agency's Lean coordinator. Attach your A3 report including any feedback from your mentor

Bibliography

Bernard, John M. *Government That Works: The Results Revolution in the States*. Results America: Thompson Shore (2015).

Bicheno, John & Holweg, Matthias. *The Lean Toolbox: A Handbook for Lean Transformation*. Fifth Edition. PICSIE Books: United Kingdom (2016).

Imai, Masaaki. *Gemba Kaizen: A Common Sense Approach to a Continuous Improvement Strategy* Second Edition. McGraw-Hill Education: New York (2012).

Manos, Anthony & Vincent, Chad, Editors. *The Lean Handbook*. ASQ Quality Press: Milwaukee, WI (2012).

Marchwinsk, Chet, Editor. *Lean Lexicon: A Graphical Glossary for Lean Thinkers*. Fifth Edition. The Lean Enterprise Institute: Cambridge, MA (2014).

Martin, Karen and Osterling, Mike. *The Kaizen Event Planner*. CRC Press Taylor and Francis Group, LLC: Boca Raton, FL (2007).

New Hampshire Bureau of Education and Training. "Lean Yellow Belt Manual" Unpublished (2018a).

New Hampshire Bureau of Education and Training. "Lean Green Belt Manual" Unpublished (2018b).

Rother, Mike. *Toyota Kata: Managing People for Improvement*, Adaptiveness and Superior Results. McGraw-Hill Education: New York (2010).

Teeuwen, Bert. *Lean for the Public Sector: The Pursuit of Perfection in Public Service*. Taylor& Francis Group, LLC, Productivity Press: New York (2011).

Womack, Jim. *Gemba Walks*. The Lean Enterprise Institute: Cambridge, MA (2011).

Index

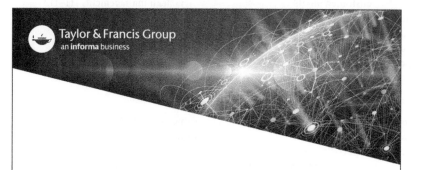

For Product Safety Concerns and Information please contact our EU
representative GPSR@taylorandfrancis.com Taylor & Francis Verlag GmbH,
Kaufingerstraße 24, 80331 München, Germany

Printed and bound by CPI Group (UK) Ltd, Croydon, CR0 4YY
01/05/2025
01858388-0001